CHANGING
FORWARD

PAUL S. MORTON

CHANGING
FORWARD

Experiencing God's Unlimited Power

Abingdon Press / *Nashville*

CHANGING FORWARD
Experiencing God's Unlimited Power

Copyright © 2012 by Paul S. Morton Sr.

This book is printed on acid-free paper.

Library of Congress Cataloging-in-Publication Data has been requested.

ISBN 978-1-4267-4135-7

All scripture quotations, unless otherwise indicated, are taken from the New King James Version®. Copyright © 1982 by Thomas Nelson, Inc. Used by permission. All rights reserved.

Scripture quotations marked KJV are from The Authorized (King James) Version. Rights in the Authorized Version in the United Kingdom are vested in the Crown. Reproduced by permission of the Crown's patentee, Cambridge University Press.

Scripture quotations marked (NIV) are taken from the Holy Bible, New International Version®, NIV®. Copyright © 1973, 1978, 1984, 2011 by Biblica, Inc.™ Used by permission of Zondervan. All rights reserved worldwide. www.zondervan.com. The "NIV" and "New International Version" are trademarks registered in the United States Patent and Trademark Office by Biblica, Inc.™

Verses marked (TLB) are taken from *The Living Bible* © 1971. Used by permission of Tyndale House Publishers, Inc., Wheaton, IL 60189. All rights reserved.

12 13 14 15 16 17 18 19 20 21—10 9 8 7 6 5 4 3 2 1

MANUFACTURED IN THE UNITED STATES OF AMERICA

CONTENTS

Contents

GOD IS WORKING CHANGE IN YOU

I n today's chaotic world the words *change* and *hope* have taken on new meanings and implications. It seems that no matter what our present circumstances may be, we tend to take some measure of comfort in things remaining "the way they are." Although we may desire change, the need to stay in our comfort zone can make us resist it—which minimizes our goals, achievements, and overall success in life.

God is always in the process of *changing us forward*: spiritually and otherwise. This is why we can have great hope for the future. We can know that as we trust and live for Him, God will keep moving us in new directions (that is, change) to fulfill our destiny and purpose. We can understand that, in everything, He's working all things together for our good.

Whether or not we are comfortable with it, change is a constant. So, let's flow forward with God's changes and we'll experience His unlimited power in our lives.

There are two levels of our struggle against change: external and internal. The greater part of this warfare is learning to see beyond external manifestations to recognize the internal—the inner person. Even those closest to you, may not be aware of your internal battle, but if you lose focus internally it can put you into bondage on both levels. This is why so many have developed a mentality of struggling against change, instead of believing God and embracing change.

Keep in mind that personal change becomes corporate change. God initiated change for the nation of Israel by first changing Moses, then Aaron, then the leaders of Israel, and then all the people. Later, He commanded Israel to possess the promised land (Canaan). Israel's acceptance of God's order to change would impact nations.

God delivered the first generation of Israelites out of Egypt, but they never saw themselves as His "change agents." They couldn't imagine their corporate role in God's process of what others would become. Because that generation stayed in bondage internally, it restricted what they were able to do externally. Accept in your mind that you are God's change agent; as you embrace your destiny, your life will impact others.

Finally, I want you to see change as a tool for spiritual growth. So, as changes come externally let them move you into deeper intimacy with God. Change comes internally when God initiates change in you, and you become His "agent of change" externally. If you keep your focus on God in the midst of change, He'll use you in ways that you could never imagine.

In spite of many challenges, God has blessed me with forward momentum, spiritual energy, and divine synergy with others for His kingdom and glory. As you read my story you will be encouraged to believe God and rise above every circumstance.

Early in life, I struggled with traditions and orthodoxy in the Pentecostal church. It was an all-consuming part of my world, and I was identified by its influence. To accept God's change I would have to renounce all the traditions I had come to know and believe. Eventually, I would even have to change geographically, which would mean severing family relationships and moving away from the people, places, and things I loved.

As I matured in my faith, it became important for me to remove any spiritual limitations that hindered me from receiving more of God. I faced many challenges during this process, but my personal change ultimately led to a corporate manifestation—forming the Full Gospel Baptist Church Fellowship (FGBCF) and the "distinctives" that give this movement its character. From its inception, the FGBCF gave others who were experiencing this same dynamic of change the right to choose. They came out of the spiritual bondage of tradition and were released into the fullness of victorious Christian living.

I thank God for "working in me" to do what was pleasing to Him even when I was rejected by clergy colleagues, when I endured a mental breakdown, and when I contended with cancer. I thank Him for girding me up during the devastation of Hurricane Katrina, when my congregation was literally dispersed nationwide. I can't express how thankful I am to the Lord for upholding me and my family when we suffered the loss of loved ones.

God is ever faithful. He has helped me focus my heart on Him in every circumstance. The losses of life can be transformed into gains for God's kingdom glory as we remain focused on Him.

Changing Forward transcends my personal legacy. It represents the story of many who are wrestling with God's call for spiritual integrity and the full manifestation of His kingdom on earth. *May I say this book relates to your story*—regardless of where you attend church, how you earn a living, and whether you are male or female, young or mature in your walk with God? I pray that as you read this book, you will embrace God's change and experience His unlimited power in your life.

CHAPTER ONE

SPIRIT OVER MIND, NOT MIND OVER SPIRIT

It was the summer of 1994 and the spiritual atmosphere was electric. We had just launched the Full Gospel Baptist Church Fellowship (FGBCF), and held our first annual conference at the Louisiana Superdome with twenty-five thousand people in attendance. God had spoken clearly and definitively: This sovereign move of His Spirit was for such a time as this.

Not long after, things started to change.

We built a dynamic team of ministers who contributed greatly to the success of this new endeavor. As time passed, however, differences of theological opinion arose in our council meetings. By and large, we were working through them and coming to an agreement; but some members couldn't get past certain church traditions. I had to stand firm because I knew what God had called me to do. God's assignment for the FGBCF was to change forward, not to retreat back into what we had always known.

About two years after starting the movement, God shook the ranks of leadership. Some of my close associates left our

1

fellowship. I started doing damage control to avoid losing other colleagues when I realized that leaving people in key roles who I knew didn't fully support the cause would ultimately result in more problems.

I realized the issue was that I didn't immediately see God's process. He had put certain people in place for a period of time to validate the movement and help get it started. It was never God's plan for *everyone* who was there in the beginning to remain.

Changing forward challenges our thinking. It requires a process of putting the truth of the Spirit over what might seem right at the time. This might be difficult, but it is a biblical concept—a spiritual mindset. In one of my favorite sermons, called *"So That,"* I explain this. The premise comes from Matthew 16:25: "For whoever desires to save his life will lose it, but whoever loses his life for My sake will find it."

Years ago I ran across a poem that flows perfectly within this premise. God gave me a strong utterance whenever I communicated it to others. Somewhat paraphrased, it says:

> I asked God for strength, that I might achieve. I was made weak, that I might learn humbly to obey. I asked for health, that I might do greater things. I was given infirmity, that I might do better things. I asked for riches, that I might be happy. I was given poverty, that I might be wise. I asked for power that I might have the praise of men. I was given weakness, that I might feel the need of God. I asked for all things that I might enjoy life. I was given life that I might enjoy all things.[1]

God adds a "so that" to our process. God permits certain things to happen in our lives "so that" we may gain insight and change forward. By the time I founded FGBCF, I had learned this well. It was time to change forward. I'm so glad that I did.

You really can't see what God wants you to see until you go through His "so that" process. Romans 8:28 clearly says: "And we know that all things work together for good to them that love God, to them who are the called according to *his* purpose" (KJV). Nothing in this life takes place by accident. God knows everything that's going to happen before it happens. He works out the "so thats" in our lives for His purpose and for our good.

Through the years, God has worked His process in me "so that" I would be prepared to step into *and* maximize every destiny assignment. I am humbled when I think back to where God has brought me and I can see now how God has worked all things together for my greater good.

Now, let's walk through my story. As we go, I pray God gives you clarity and victory in your own "so that" process.

I continuously give thanks to God for the blessing of my three children. Jasmine, my oldest daughter, really loves the Lord and became one of the greatest church administrators a senior pastor could have. She was always focused and had finesse in dealing with people and handling the business of church. My only son, P. J., is a gifted musician and singer and has an uncanny drive for perfection. Christiann, my younger daughter, is so special to me. Her creative mind and technical use of graphics has positioned her for greatness in several areas. Each of them has continuously been a blessing to our family.

Jasmine is married to Elvin Ross, a musical producer for many of the Tyler Perry plays and films. They have two sons, Elvin Jr. and London Paul, and evidence is clear that I love them more than words can say. P. J. is married to Kortni and they have two sons, JaKai and Paul Morton III. Christy is unmarried but would probably tie the knot immediately, if she didn't know that her allowance would be discontinued. I think she's almost ready but I still consider her my "spoiled baby."

We have a solid and stable fun-loving family and because of the combination of my seriousness about things and my wife's humor, the family has balance. Much of that family stability and balance were shaken in March, 2003, after my Wednesday Night Bible Study in New Orleans. I received a call from Jasmine and Elvin, who were residing in Atlanta with my precious granddaughter, Kai. At eighteen months old, she was my only grandchild. She was just beginning to talk. When they would visit New Orleans or we went to Atlanta, she would always jump up in my arms, calling me, "Papa" and calling my wife, "GiGi." She was my heart. She made herself at home in our house and knowing where our bedroom was located, she would push the door open without knocking. With her, we were on top of the world and we always had the expectation of getting a call from them at night, telling us about what she had done that day.

The call that night from Jasmine was alarmingly different. We were already in bed and I could tell something was wrong from her voice. Her words are imprinted even now in my mind: "Dad, Dad, pray! I'm in my car, taking Kai to the hospital. She's not responding. Daddy, her lips are turning blue. Pray, Daddy, pray!" Her frantic pleas for my prayers and my desire for God to intervene literally collided. With them at the Atlanta hospital emergency room, my wife and I walked and prayed and prayed and walked, determined to remove the effects of what we would have rather believed to have been a bad dream. It wasn't a bad dream.

It was too late to catch a commercial flight to Atlanta, so we chartered a plane. I was praying, "Lord, if I could just get to my grandbaby and hold her and pray for her in my arms." It was too late. Jasmine called as we were getting ready to fly and told me the three hardest words that I could ever hear: "Daddy, she's gone." Kai had died from a virus that could not have been prevented from its path of destruction in her body.

I had experienced the intense emotional pain of losing a father, mother, and sister, but there was no replicate pain like this in my history. I asked God to help me through the moment, not just for me, but for my family. Though my children were grown, they were still at the level of believing that "Daddy can get us out of anything!" I had been the "strong daddy," but at this point I felt weak and helpless. This was more than grief and bereavement. These feelings exacted great remorse and inner conflict.

Through my ministry gifts, I had comforted thousands of people, but this one was extremely hard on me. My wife and I cried many days together in what seemed our weakest moments, but we realized we had to be just as strong together. Our pain was perhaps compounded and seemed almost unbearable because of its effect on Jasmine and Elvin. The knowledge of their pain was even more difficult.

How It All Began

I was born in Windsor, Ontario, Canada, to Clarence and Matilda Morton. At the time of my birth, my father was fifty-three years old—twenty-three years older than my mother. We lived right across the river from Detroit, Michigan. These two cities were near to each other geographically, but they were very different culturally. There were about two hundred thousand people living in Windsor, with only 1 percent of the population being African Canadian. In contrast, the City of Detroit had a population of more than 1.5 million and was predominantly African American, Thousands of

African Americans had migrated there from the South to find jobs in the automotive plants, which resulted in the proliferation of great African American churches and pastors, as well as the R&B (that is, Motown) music industry.

I was the seventh of nine Morton siblings. I had three brothers: Clarence Jr., George, and James; and five sisters: Ruby, Nancy, Gwendolyn, Jacqueline, and Jeanetta. (We're all still trying to figure out how our parents made it with that many children in the house at the same time.) My brothers and sisters thought I was "spoiled" because they say I got away with so much. They viewed me as his "baby boy," since I was the youngest son. I think this was probably more their imagination than fact.

Our father was an anointed preacher, an effective leader, and a prophet. I was told that after I was born, he held me up before his congregation and told them he was giving me the name "Paul" because I would be a "great preacher." He had prophesied the preaching anointing on all of his sons. Our father wanted each one of us to preach, but I received the gift of the prophetic office.

There was balance in the Morton household. Our mother had a very strong temperament, a firm hand, and was the primary disciplinarian. She didn't play around. It seemed Proverbs 13:24 was our parents' motto: "He who spares his rod hates his son, but he who loves him disciplines him promptly." They never failed to activate this verse when our behavior warranted it.

Low self-esteem was forbidden. We could never use the excuse with our parents that someone "didn't like us" or was "smarter than us." They insisted that we were Mortons and to conduct ourselves accordingly. Now, don't get me wrong. We didn't use our family name as an excuse to defy authority; nor did we see ourselves as being better than others. We did, however, develop a deep sense of family pride. Our parents instilled many strong values in us and demonstrated to us daily how we should live our lives with excellence.

An Abiding Spiritual Legacy

Our father was a recognized visionary. Born in the 1800s, he was denied a formal education but was given a miraculous gift of reading. The Lord called him to preach at age sixteen. Since he couldn't read, our father fasted and prayed for days with his face in the Bible, and when he raised his head he could read. He went to his mother, read aloud to her, and asked whether he had read the text correctly. With astonishment, she replied, *"Yes!"*

From the day he was called to preach, our father would teach and preach to anyone he met. Ultimately, he memorized the majority of the Bible.

Miracles like the one God performed for my father are seldom understood, but they can't be disputed. God will equip and use whomever He chooses. He sovereignly gives His chosen vessels whatever they may lack to ensure His work is accomplished. God gave my father what he could not have obtained otherwise at the time He surrendered to preach. Now, that's a powerful "so that" testimony! God is able to take people others dismiss as being without value and make them prominent.

When God calls you and activates His anointing in your life, you don't get to choose whether or not you're able to carry out His assignment. Moses was a perfect example of this. At first, he tried to tell God he couldn't deliver the Israelites out of Egypt. God didn't take *no* for an answer. He sovereignly gave Moses what he needed to get the job done. (Read Exodus 3:1–4:17.) God did the same thing for my father, and He'll do it for you and me.

By the Lord's mighty hand, my father became the pastor of "one church in two locations," actually, in two countries, Canada and America. Eventually, he planted more than thirteen churches (in both countries) during his lifetime.

All of the Morton children learned to respect the "man of God"— the preacher. When other preachers came to town, our parents invited them to stay in our home. Because of this, we interacted with some of the greatest church leaders who had ever lived.

Bishop C. H. Mason, founder of the Church of God in Christ (which became one of the largest Pentecostal movements in history) was a frequent visitor in our home. Our parents would always call upon him to lead us in prayer at the dining table before meals. Bishop Mason prayed long prayers. Some of them were so long that my mother had to reheat the food before we could eat it. Yet, we learned to sit silently until he concluded prayer.

Being a preacher's kid (PK) definitely has its challenges. People expected more of us, and we were compelled to rise to the expectations of others. Baseball games and movies weren't part of our upbringing. He feared that if we were good at sports, we might become professional athletes and miss our calling as ministers.

You could say the Morton siblings had a unique childhood "so that" we could ultimately carry on our father's work. That was his dream and vision. Eventually, his heart's desire came to pass.

CHAPTER TWO

CHOOSING TO MAKE
THINGS BETTER

No matter how good or bad your situation may be, you can always choose to make things better. By the grace of God, this ethic has been part of me for as long as I can remember. I had good and bad days, but my foundation was good. God had placed seeds of destiny in me, and He's done the same for you.

When I was in elementary school, one of my white friends got angry with me and called me the "N-word." I wanted so badly to hit him, but didn't. Instead, I felt I could straighten him out with my "smart English." I told him, almost as if I were preaching, "Look at my skin. God had me in 'Heaven's oven' and I'm 'well-done.' Look at you. God didn't finish you. You're only 'half done.' God didn't have time to finish you." I was surprised when he started crying, and through his tears said, "I want to be like you."

The only black student in my class, I soon found out that most of my white friends wanted to "be like me." One day during recess, my friend and five other boys were lying on the ground trying to get "well-done"—like me. They were so serious about it that one of their parents came to the school and asked, "Who is this Paul Morton who told my child he 'wasn't done,' and convinced my child that he could be his color?"

I was summoned to the principal's office, along with the classmate who had called me the "N-word." As I left, I heard one of my teachers say, "Now, that's a powerful fellow!" I was in fifth grade, about ten years old, when I first realized I had the potential to bring about change.

Another time, during music class, I took over the classroom when the teacher had briefly left the room. Without her permission, I sat down at the piano. Someone else went to the drums, and we started a "jam session." When the teacher returned, she knew I had been the ringleader and immediately sent me to the principal's office for disrupting the class.

I knew the routine. That meant I would get three "straps" (hits) on each hand. I had been through all the possible "strapping" categories before. I was determined to take it like a man.

However, on this day the principal didn't follow the same routine. They told me that my teacher had decided to call my father. I panicked and screamed: "No! Please don't do that!" Apparently, they thought my father was going to discipline me over the phone. My dad talked with me for a few minutes, and then told the teacher to send me home.

Since we lived twelve blocks from the school, she asked if he was going to pick me up. Emphatically he replied, "No!" When I got home my dad called the teacher, and then he took off his belt and "went to town" on me. I knew not to act tough when he was punishing me. The tougher we acted, the longer he used the belt. He wanted to see and hear us cry. I cried! I hollered, even before he touched me, "I'm sorry, Daddy. I won't do it anymore! Please, Daddy. I'm sorry!"

When he was finished, my father picked up the phone again and said, "He's on his way back now. Good-bye!" By the time I walked back I really was fine, but my teacher was waiting. She ran to me with open arms, "Oh, I'm so sorry," she said. "Are you all right?" I went into acting mode, pretending to cry. I slowly lifted my eyes and asked, "Why did you send me home?" She never called my father again.

So, my gift of leadership had surfaced, but there was obviously still some work to do. I'm sure you can remember times when you flowed in your gifts and your calling without realizing it. Are you still changing forward, maximizing the abilities He has given you.

My older brothers were in a singing group at church. Every time I tried to join in, they'd push me aside. Then I'd cry to my father, and he'd make them include me in the group. They got so angry with me they ultimately stopped using the name The Morton Brothers and formed a new group with two other members. They called themselves The Progressive Singers.

What do you do when something that's working for others isn't working for you? Create! Although I really wanted to be part of my brothers' group, I decided to create my own. So, I looked for the best singers in the church and started The Junior Progressives. I took it a step further and, adding a few more friends, created a community group called The Untouchables. I began to understand how important it is to develop team relationships. During the summer months, we did various chores for the elderly, who never failed to give us at least a quarter for cutting the grass. Of course, we didn't report the "earnings" to my father.

With plenty of snowy winters in Canada, we soon knew the places where cars would most often get stuck. Stranded owners would have to call a tow truck to get them out, which was usually very expensive. We got the idea that The Untouchables could become the alternative to the tow truck monopoly, and we developed our own techniques for pulling cars out of the snow. Then we hung around those "trouble spots" and were right there to provide a cheaper option.

We made good money until one day a member of my father's church got stuck in the heavy snow and didn't want to pay for having his car removed. As far as he was concerned, I was the preacher's kid, and I shouldn't charge a fee to a church member for doing a good deed. To me, this wasn't a good deed; it was business! Of course, I had to pay for that remark when he told my father about my little enterprise. I think I lost much of my passion for creative entrepreneurship after that incident.

In order to redeem myself with my parents, each of The Untouchables had to assist a family in the church without charging. I was assigned to carry the groceries of an elderly widow. She was kind and asked me to stay for a bite to eat. That was fine, until she set three places at the table, one for her, one for me, and one for her dead husband—who she spoke to as if he had joined us. That scared me to death.

I realized that I had leadership potential, even though at times I suffered because of it.

A Moment of Change with My Father

When I was about twelve years old my father came to me and said, "Son, come on, just you and me—let's go for a ride." We had never done that before! I was so proud he had invited me that I went out of my way to tell my brothers and sisters about it—and that they couldn't come with us.

After riding around together for a while, my father pulled the car over and said: "Son, you're special. God let me have you in my old age because He has something special for you to do. I'm not going to be here forever, but you and the family must carry on." He continued talking and suddenly paused. He grabbed my hands, looked me straight in the eyes and said: "Promise me that you will listen to what I am saying. You remind me so much of me."

Wow! It felt so good to hear him say those words. Just as calmly, he said: "Now this is just between you and me, all right?" "Yes, sir," I replied. That day, he prayed for me like no other time I could remember. I truly believe that's when God passed my father's powerful mantle to me. I suppose he knew he was dying and that I would need the most encouragement.

My father passed away that year. He was sixty-five years old. The doctor told us he died of "natural causes," but that he had "the body of a ninety-year-old man." Hard work without adequate rest had taken my father's life. I would remember this lesson in my later years.

My father's passing was very difficult for me. I couldn't understand why death had taken him from me.

I shut down. I didn't want to go to school. Having lost my father, school seemed far less important to me. My grief seemed so much greater than anything I could gain in my classes.

I was mad at God! My dad was a good man who loved my mother, his family, and the church. He was my hero. Now that he was gone, everything was different. My two older brothers, C. L. and George, had taken over pastoring the churches in Windsor, Ontario, and Detroit, Michigan, respectively. C. L. was twenty and George was nineteen when they assumed those roles; George had one of the largest church memberships in Windsor.

My mother kept reminding me of who I was, reassuring me that my father was fine. She told me that the best thing I could do was to carry on his legacy. He had empowered me to change the world. Though it was painful, I embraced the process of changing forward.

I don't know your story, but I'm certain you've had to overcome setbacks to get to where you are today: maybe even the loss of a loved one. No matter what may come, your gifts and calling from God are in you. Immaturity or trouble won't keep them from surfacing. Being angry at God won't even abort them, as long as you don't give up and walk away from Him. I pray you settle this between you and the Lord right now, "so that" you will live the life He has for you.

CHAPTER THREE

O, THAT I
HAD WINGS!

A few years later, God started dealing with me about my calling. At that same time, my mother started challenging me to pull myself together and get more focused. My father's words had never left me. Since our time together in the car, I had been prepared to be a change agent; I just wasn't ready yet to accept God's calling for my life.

I had been born with a hernia. My father had prayed for me when I was an infant and claimed my healing. As I grew older he'd pull me aside and pray for me. His faith kept my faith strong. Then when my father went home to be with the Lord, I let go of claiming my healing.

Having the hernia got me out of chores that I didn't want to do. There was nothing wrong with me and I would laugh to myself. This didn't sit well with my siblings because they knew better.

But they got me back. I was walking a beautiful girl home after school, determined to impress her by carrying her books. When my brother came up behind us and excitedly yelled, "Oh, no! My brother can't carry your books; he can't carry anything. He has a hernia!"

Even I was almost convinced that I might have collapsed if I walked a step farther. My brother's facial expression and tone of voice were spot on. I tried to redeem myself by saying, "Stop it. That's not true!" But it was too late. Now, on the one hand my brother messed up my impressing that girl. On the other hand I was delivered from ever complaining about carrying heavy grocery bags again.

The truth always catches up and outlasts a lie. I couldn't see it then, but God was working in me through His "so that" process.

Making Ends Meet

While my father was alive, he supported our family well, and our mother didn't have to work outside the home. Though we didn't have any financial worries, he had used much of his pastoral compensation to benefit the churches he had founded. When our father passed away there were six children under the age of sixteen living at home. We all had to help.

My brother James was one of the greatest musicians around and played for several of the leading churches in the area. I was about fifteen years old and realized I had a gift for excellence. I got a job shining shoes at Charlie's Shoe Clinic after school and on Saturdays.

If I was going to shine shoes, I wanted to be the best at it. I became so good at shining shoes that customers came in and asked for me. Business doubled. Shoes were stacked up around the shop. I made sure I wasn't merely an average shoe-shine boy. Think about it. When you are average, you're only at "the top of the bottom."

Our mother had always been wise with the family resources, but after dad's passing she became extremely frugal. She frequently talked about how tough times had become. Yet, she still had a great deal of personal and family pride. To help meet some of the household needs, I slipped money in her purse without her knowing it.

She ultimately figured out what was going on and one day called me in and said, "Son, I know the Lord is good—but is this you?" This was another "so that" lesson for me. I wasn't going to lie to my mother. She wasn't angry, but she told me to use the money I earned for myself. Knowing I couldn't be of help to her that way anymore, I figured out other ways to be a blessing. I firmly believe that "seeding into" her life is one of the main reasons I am blessed today.

Yielding to My Calling

People often ask me how I knew I was called to preach. I can tell you that I didn't see a white cloud in the sky with words "Go Preach" embroidered on the side or a man riding a white horse carrying a sign. There was just a "pressing" in my mind that ultimately became so strong I knew it wasn't me, nor could it be the devil.

Anytime God is dealing with major situations in your life, there's going to be spiritual warfare and competition with the mind. By the time I turned sixteen, I knew God was preparing me for something greater. When I finally acknowledged God's calling, my mind immediately said, *I don't want to do this* but God was saying, "Do it."

Around that time my brother C. L. asked me to direct his church choir. He had been extremely successful since taking over our father's church as pastor. I came on board and was perfectly satisfied with what he had me doing. God had me in that "so that" process for about three years. Every now and then I would remind myself that I didn't want to preach; I wanted to meet girls, and I was thoroughly convinced they didn't want anything to do with teenage preachers.

Singing was my passion. Then one day while I was singing a lead part, my voice started cracking. It was terrible! No matter what I did, it continued. The pressure on me to sing well increased. The greatest critiques came from my family, but there was also pressure outside my family. With those pressures mounting , I had no choice. I was desperate. I told the Lord that if He would give me back my voice, I would preach.

By confronting my issues and exposing what was in my heart and mind, God was challenging me to change forward. It was time for me to acknowledge and accept my calling, so my destiny would unfold the way He intended. I was definitely uncomfortable while God was pressing in on me from every side, but His process was working "all things together" for my good.

I want you to keep this in mind as you walk through your own "so that" process. For me, it was only the beginning. I'm sure the same has been true for you. We have to stay focused on the Lord and have faith that He's not going to give up on us—even when His "so that" process exposes flaws in our thinking or character. God's thoughts and ways are much higher than ours. The next time the Lord is "pressing" you to change, remember His word always accomplishes His purpose. (See Isaiah 55:6-11.) Are you doing what God has called you to do for His glory?

My First Sermon

Both C. L. and George had already established themselves as great pulpiteers. Up to that point, my brother James always stubbornly said, "I ain't preaching." He finally conceded and accepted his calling. It became apparent to people on both sides of the U.S.-Canada border that the Morton name was synonymous with "great preachers."

When the "pressing" of God became so heavy on me that I couldn't eat, sleep, or rest, I finally surrendered to God's calling. My first sermon was, "O That I Had Wings!" I guess I was preaching out of my own experience, because if I had wings, I would have flown away from what God had called me to do—but He had made it crystal clear to me that I had to take His calling on my life seriously.

My brother C. L. was both my pastor and mentor and kept me close to him during my years of development as a preacher. I continued to serve as his choir director, as well as his "armor bearer" (personal assistant). I made sure everything was in order, so he could focus on preaching the word of God.

To become a good preacher—or to undertake any role in God's kingdom—one must commit to being a good servant. Always remember: the only way to the throne room is through the servants' quarters. There are would-be leaders who want to go right to the top in ministry without spending any time learning the ins and outs of being a servant. My counsel is to embrace humility, fellowship with others, and seek the common good over trying to get ahead personally. We must stand strong in spiritual warfare and fight the "good fight" of faith! Jesus humbled himself and became a servant, to the point that He embraced death on the cross. My counsel to you, as God gives you opportunities to serve, is to thank Him for giving you this same mindset, "which was also in Christ Jesus" (Philippians 2:5).

There were many times when God was dealing with me about my calling that I wanted to spread my wings and fly away. That was before I fully submitted myself to the Lord. Once I accepted my calling and became a willing servant, God helped me to excel in doing the things that were required of me. We can't escape change, but we can choose to trust God and flow with His process. God is changing us forward. Our attitude, our willingness to serve God and others, determines whether we will get bitter or better.

CHAPTER FOUR

THE LEGACY OF A PREACHING FATHER

I firmly believe that the destiny of each Morton sibling stemmed from our father's anointing and personal influence in our lives. He prophesied that we would each be actively engaged in ministry and in the church. This ultimately happened as he had spoken. Each of the Morton siblings has served the Lord in our respective venues as preachers, singers, or church administrators. Truly, God's blessing in our lives is connected to our father's love for and submission to the Lord.

Clarence Morton Sr. served God, our family, and others with the utmost of integrity. I remember our mother telling us how our father would come home, and while we were sleeping, anoint us with oil and pray that we would never be an embarrassment to God or to him.

Our parents trained us up to be people of integrity and to surround ourselves with people of integrity. He also told us that the people we would lead should follow us because they believe in us.

Our family was not immune to difficulties. One of my brothers was pressed into leading a large church when he was too young and immature. He fell into sin with a woman in the congregation. Our mother insisted he step down. This mistake broke his heart, and he turned to a life of drugs. I have not seen that brother in more than thirty years, but I pray for him every day.

There is a lesson to be learned: never sell your present for your future. There are people today who are either in jail or addicted to drugs because they became so wrapped up in the present, they forgot their future.

If God has called you into the ministry, it is very important for you to be properly prepared. Our father was a proven leader.

A pastor must have a certain degree of maturity. He or she must undergo a process of training and orientation before taking on the responsibilities of ministry. During his time, our father didn't have the resources at his disposal that we now enjoy, so God did a sovereign work both in and through him. Now, there are churches, Bible schools, and ministry programs around the world that are available to anyone. God may have called you, like me, into ministry as a teenager, but you must come through His process of preparation. You should submit yourself to training "so that" you can build the work God wants to establish through you. In our church, we prepare our ministers to take the next step in their lives and ministry. I firmly believe that, beyond seminary, pastors need mentors—seasoned leaders who will train them until they are ready to be fully released.

More Tough Family Transitions

Our mother became ill when I was around nineteen years old. As I sat by her bedside, seeing her painfully dying from cancer, I asked the Lord to take her. She had suffered so much trying to keep the family together. In what became the final moments of her time with us, I whispered in her ear, "You will be fine." Then she quietly went away.

I learned so much from my mother. She had been an excellent example of servanthood. I don't know how she did it all. Matilda Elizabeth Morton was a tremendous gift from God, so helpful and faithful at serving others.

After our mother went to be with the Lord, I continued living in the family home with my two younger sisters and took on the responsibility of being head of the household. I determined to remain focused on the fact that we were family, and regardless of our mistakes, we had to continue loving and caring for each other. That was the "Morton Way."

Growing in My Calling

A year later I was named co-pastor with my brother C. L. at the church in Windsor, Ontario, where he basically left me in charge. When he became a bishop, he sent me to pastor a church in Chatman, Ontario. I was about twenty-one years old at that time. C. L. had witnessed how the church in Windsor had grown, and wanted me to do the same thing in Chatman, about sixty miles away from Windsor. It was there that I learned and lived Matthew 18:20, in which Jesus said: "where two or three are gathered together in My name, I am there in the midst of them." It was a tiny church, much different from what I had known.

The church in Chatman was literally a one-man operation. I had to open and close the church, do the janitorial work, and handle anything else that needed to be done. Remembering that my father had named me "Paul" because I was going to be a great preacher, I couldn't resist asking, "Lord, is this it?"

I was determined, however, to give it my best. Your success in life, especially if you are called to be a leader, depends on your willingness to submit to leadership. Being faithful in the small things is a big part of God's "so that" process. Pastoring in Chatman was a hard lesson, but I learned it.

In the eyes of the Lord, obedience is better than sacrifice (see 1 Samuel 15:22b). When you are humble and obedient, God richly blesses you.

This reminds me of another situation at a church where my brother James, who had accepted his calling after I received mine, was being considered as the pastor—True Faith Baptist Church in Detroit. One Sunday, James couldn't make it to preach as part of their considera- tion process. He had a prior commitment and sent me to preach for him. James instructed me to find the church's chairman of deacons and let him know that he had sent me. When I found the chairman, he looked at me and said, "I don't know who sent you, but you're not preaching here." I was shocked! That was my first encounter with a Baptist church, and it didn't feel good at all.

I left the premises with no intention of returning.

We had grown up in the Pentecostal church. When the pastor (our father) said something, people listened. It was different at True Faith; the board totally ran the church.

In every situation, God was preparing me for something greater. We often learn where we really stand when we are tested; it's all part of the Lord's "so that" process. Remember this the next time God permits a difficult situation to unfold in your life. He chal- lenges our thinking "so that" we may gain insight, change forward, and fulfill our destiny. I thank God that through every challenge, His "changing forward" process is an everyday reality in our lives.

CHAPTER FIVE

SO NEW TO ME

After finishing a Wednesday night Bible study at my brother's church in Detroit, a dear woman, approached me and spoke a prophetic word into my life. She pulled me aside and said, "Paul, God showed me something about you. He showed you as pastor of a big church with thousands of members. I know your family likes to remain close but God has shown me that your destiny is not in this city. You will move far away. When God tells me something, it always comes true. So, you pray over what I've said."

Needless to say, her words disturbed me greatly. The conversation in the car with my father years before echoed in my mind. I had heard what she said about moving, but there was nothing in my own thoughts or experiences that came anywhere close to it. Out of respect for her as an elderly church mother, I thanked her and promised to be prayerful.

Of course, the prophecy wasn't immediately fulfilled. I continued to preach wherever I was asked. I was conducting a week-long revival in Cleveland, Ohio, about three hundred miles from Windsor. In order to "look the part" of an evangelist, I bought several suits at one of those stores where one could get any suit in any color for $29.95. I was confident that I would be "sharply attired" for all the meetings.

I was speaking in an old-fashioned Church of God in Christ (COGIC) revival, which guaranteed a powerful move of the Holy Spirit every night. We sang, prayed, and sought the Presence of God all week. On the final night, I planned to leave right after the service and parked my packed car in a reserved space in front of the church.

At the end of the evening, I came outside and found *no car* and *none of my suits*. To make matters worse, being young and foolish, I also hadn't purchased car insurance.

Totally upset, I ran back inside, screaming, "Somebody stole my car!" Some of the older church mothers were still in the building and immediately began praising God, speaking in tongues, and declaring the devil was mad because the Lord had blessed the revival. It took every ounce of respect I could muster to hold back what I was thinking.

I hadn't yet reached the level of spiritual maturity where I understood God's "so that" process and could declare Romans 8:28: "And we know that all things work together for good to them that love God, to them who are the called according to *his* purpose" (KJV). I didn't understand that I might have experienced this loss "so that" I could gain greater riches in Christ.

I managed to get home the next day and told my story. I even preached about it in my sermon that Sunday, but nobody offered to help me recoup from losing the car or the suits. I was beside myself. I had given my best to God's people, but it seemed like I was the only one who recognized the value of my contributions.

I reasoned that I had been a good "church boy" all my life and for nothing. I decided to leave my home, family and ministry and begin again somewhere else. Now, listen closely. If you are in ministry, be careful not to get caught up in external appearances. You could lose sight of the calling and anointing that is upon you and get out of step with God.

An Unexpected Opportunity

A few depression-filled days later, I boarded a Greyhound bus to Atlanta, Georgia, found a one-room apartment for about thirty dollars a week, and got a job selling encyclopedias. I did very well.

One evening, my coworkers invited me to go to a nightclub. I was twenty-two, but I had never been to a nightclub; in fact, I'd never had a drink of liquor in my life. This was a whole new world. I ordered ginger ale, but even that was too strong for me.

Loud music and nonstop conversations were going on all around us. The room was filled with smoke, which made the already dimly lit space seem darker. I tried to blend in because everyone else seemed to be having a good time.

It was Talent Night at the club. My friends had heard me singing to myself at work, so they said, "Morton, why don't you get up there and sing?" "No," I replied emphatically. They insisted. I almost felt obligated to comply since I had come as their guest. Plus, I think I also wanted to show them I was "cool."

I was miles away from the Canadian border. Who would know? I went on stage. The only secular song I really knew was "Betcha by Golly Wow" by the Stylistics. When I finished my rendition, the audience applauded and called for more.

Unknown to me, there was a talent scout in the crowd. He came over after my impromptu performance, introduced himself, and told me that I had what it took to take my talent to the next level. I was shocked and excited.

I really was all alone. This nightclub in Atlanta was definitely another world, far removed from the churches in Windsor and Chatman. The possibility of a "new tomorrow" hinged on my response to a music industry representative I had never met and who was promising a glimmer of future success.

I started rationalizing within myself, becoming more practical than spiritual. Deep down, I could tell my mind was operating over my spirit, rather than my spirit ruling my mind. Thinking back, I know the devil was trying to make me miss my destiny: preaching and leading God's people. He wanted me to change backward.

Don't get me wrong. I don't have anything against people who sing clean love songs. Years later, my only son, P. J., wanted to write some good music that young people could sing and enjoy. While he was developing the lyrics he asked me, "If God is love and love is God, why can't we sing about love?" It took me a minute to realize how correct and on point he was. As long as he kept "love" within the boundaries of the word of God, he had the right to sing good, clean, and inspiring love songs.

My father's prophecy was still being reconciled within me. Mother Aretha's prophecy had yet to be fulfilled, but I decided to move forward, entangled in a spirit of rebellion to the words God had released over my life.

I took the talent scout's card and gave him my contact information. A few days later, he called and I met him at the home of a music producer from a major record label. The house was huge and had a big sound studio. The producer asked me to sing. He wanted me to show him my "raw talent." Again I sang "Betcha by Golly Wow," "Yes!" he exclaimed. "You are the voice we've been looking for. You will be famous and rich. Just stick with me." With that, he confidently placed one hand on my shoulder and shook my hand with the other, as if to seal the deal.

This whole situation was moving too fast for me. It was difficult to keep up with the conversations and strategic plans for production and marketing that the record company executives were putting together right before my eyes. Because I was a new talent, they wanted me to sing a song with a then famous female vocalist whose popularity had declined. They thought I could help reignite her career while launching my own.

After the two of us rehearsed, everyone declared the arrangement would be a big hit! The producer, the talent scout, and other executives were all ecstatic. They could "smell the money" coming to all of us.

One of the people there announced, "This is a good guy. He's out of the church and a preacher. He sings gospel, too." (That, of course, wasn't uncommon. Many singers in the secular music industry are products of the church and love singing a good "church song.") I asked the studio musician if he knew "Walk Around Heaven All Day." He knew the melody and started playing. I flowed right in:

> One of these mornings, won't be very long
> You will look for me and I'll be gone.[1]

As I sang, my father flashed before my eyes; everything I had been taught suddenly came back to me. I realized that although I was angry, one day I'd be going to Glory. I thought, *Do I want to go "home" to heaven outside of my destiny?* Right then and there, I came to terms again with the fact there was a greater calling on my life. I started to cry. Straining to look through my own tears, I saw that everyone else in the room was crying as well. I couldn't help it; I yelled out: "I can't do this! I have to preach!"

Deafening silence filled the air. If I hadn't already seen the others in the studio, I would have thought I was all alone in that place.

I was baffled. A "church song" had just mesmerized these entertainment professionals who had been swaying and swooning over an R&B duet a few minutes earlier. Now, there was an eerie stillness. But soon the silence was broken; they all started cursing me out! I hadn't ever heard some of the words they used against me, not even in Detroit. It was the first time I ever let someone curse me out without saying a word.

I thank God that I was shaken back into the reality of my calling. Those people had seen *their* destiny in me, *not mine*. God had called me to preach and too many prophecies had been spoken over my life for me to go in another direction.

This was much more than a failed business opportunity. It was major spiritual warfare. God had a destiny for me, but I was rushing His plan when I went to Atlanta. That day, God put His hand on me and re-routed me back home—where He would soon reveal my next step.

It's clear in the Bible that patience is a virtue (see Hebrews 12:1-2 and James 1:2-4). If you know God has called you to do a work, you need to wait on His timing. Your destiny assignment isn't likely to come as quickly as you would like; but rest assured, God has a perfect time for you to change forward. Hear me. *You don't have to force God's agenda.* If your calling hasn't fully manifested, wait for your time of release and don't rush it. God will work everything out in His timing for His purpose and for your good.

Getting Back on Track

I returned to Canada determined to wait on the Lord. As I waited and served, I prayed, "Lord, I'm sorry. I know You didn't want me to be an R&B singer—You called me to preach. Where do You want me to go?"

Change was in the air.

The Call to New Orleans

A couple of months after returning home, I clearly heard the voice of God in my spirit. There was no doubt: He wanted me to relocate to New Orleans, Louisiana. This calling was strange to me. I didn't know anybody there! Nevertheless, I said, "Lord, If You say go, I'm going to go."

It was hard for me to be the first Morton to permanently move away from the rest of the family, but I felt God had been as direct with me as He had been with Abraham when He said to him: "Get out of your country, from your family and from your father's house, to a land I will show you." (See Genesis 12:1.)

Now, I didn't have a car, and I only had one suit. With a little money in my pocket, I bought another Greyhound bus ticket— this time for the long ride to New Orleans—a place I had never been, to meet people I had never known, and to do something I had never done. I told only my brother James before I left, fearing the rest of the family would do everything they could to make me stay.

It's often difficult to see what God is doing as we're going through His "so that" process. I can only say that God lets circumstances and events occur in your life to assure you won't miss your scheduled destiny and purpose.

Obey the counsel of Proverbs 3:5-6 "so that" you can move into your destiny: "Trust in the Lord with all your heart, and lean not on your own understanding; in all your ways acknowledge Him, and He shall direct your paths." I was learning this lesson very well.

CHAPTER SIX

I SEE GREATER

It was November 1972 when I arrived at my destination. Knowing my budget wouldn't allow me to stay long at the hotel I had checked into near the bus station, I found a one-room apartment in Uptown New Orleans. The neighborhood wasn't exclusive by any stretch of the imagination, but it was my new home. When you're changing forward, you often have to crawl before you walk.

I had $800 to get a car that could get me around the city. I found a 1959 Buick. It was huge, burned a lot of gasoline, and looked like something my grandfather would have driven, but it worked.

The first thing on my mind was finding a church home. The second place I visited was Greater St. Stephen Missionary Baptist Church. It was within walking distance from my apartment, so I figured I couldn't lose anything by checking it out. As soon as I entered the sanctuary, God spoke to my spirit that this was the place where He was sending me. That Sunday, a visiting pastor brought the message. After he had finished giving a great sermon, he extended the invitation to discipleship. I was more than ready to join.

Since this was my first time in the South and in that church, I followed the flow of the people—out of the church. I had no idea these were the disobedient ones who wanted to leave early. Innocently, I had followed the wrong crowd and missed my opportunity for church membership. I learned that they had an evening service, and I was determined to return and join.

That night, Greater St. Stephen was having "Baptist Training Union" (BTU). I was used to attending "full-blown" night services with choirs singing, powerful preaching, and so on. Only a few people were attending this service, but I felt a connection there. As it turned out, I couldn't join that night either. The rule for joining the church was that a vote had to be taken, and it could only be initiated by the pastor (who wasn't there).

In an attempt to avoid discouraging me, they took my name and asked me to sit in front. I had told them I was a minister back home in Canada, so they asked me to give a testimony. (In a way, this reminded me of my experience at the nightclub where I was persuaded to perform.) I stood and shared how unusual it was for me to immediately take the step toward becoming a member. I shared that I knew God had brought me to that place, that I was certain I had heard His voice. I told them, although I didn't know anyone in New Orleans, I felt right at home at Greater St. Stephen. When I finished, the congregation was shouting and praising God. It was obvious the love of God was in this church; everyone was so kind. I was impressed with Southern hospitality!

The next opportunity to join the church was on the upcoming Sunday, which happened to be the week of Thanksgiving. That day couldn't come too soon for me. When I arrived, the church (which could seat at least five hundred people) was filled, and they were "on fire" for God. As soon as the pastor entered the sanctuary, he said, "I understand a young preacher joined our church on Sunday night at BTU. Is he here?"

Scared and trembling, I stood up; he called me up to the front. People began applauding vigorously as I approached him in the pulpit. He asked, "Why are you sitting out there? You should have come to the pulpit." I was a little disturbed by that remark, because my father had always told us it was better to be "asked up" than to be "asked down." I didn't want to tell him my real reason for sitting with the congregation: I was about to join a church in which I had never heard the preacher say a word until that moment. This was definitely a "God thing!"

The Reverend Percy Simpson preached that morning, and his message was very good. In fact, he was known as a great preacher and pastor. After the message, he extended the invitation and asked me to come down front, so they could officially "vote me in" as a member. Then he asked me to give a testimony. I shared again how God had brought me from Windsor, Ontario, Canada to New Orleans.

The same thing happened—the church erupted in shouting. Finally, since he couldn't stop them, Pastor Simpson shouted over the people, "Would y'all like to hear this young man preach next Sunday?" They resounded, "Yes, Lord! Yes!"

From that first day, Pastor Simpson began to mentor me. Finding a "father" like him was gratifying. Soon his wife, Lillie Mae Simpson, was like a mother to me, and their children were like my brothers and sisters. I called him Pastor Simpson out of respect for his position as senior pastor, but he insisted that I call him "Papa" Simpson.

Greater Things Unfolding

The following Sunday I preached the first sermon God gave me a second time, "O That I Had Wings." Now, my understanding of this word was even greater. To walk in the purpose of God, we need to be where He wants us to be, when He wants us to be there, doing what He wants us to do—even if He leads us completely outside our comfort zone.

The congregation's response amazed me; I had never received one quite like it. I could feel the confirmation of God's message and the change that was taking place in my life. His peace came over me. After that day, many doors opened up for me at Greater St. Stephen and at other churches in the city. It wasn't long before I was preaching three and four times every Sunday somewhere. It was as if the word of the Lord over my life was coming to pass at an accelerated pace.

People had loved me in Canada, but God was blessing me on an even greater level here. Sometimes, it was difficult to keep my feet on the ground. I had to ask God to keep me humble.

About two weeks after I joined the church, a girl caught my eye. Her name was Debra Brown and she was eighteen years old. She was beautiful, classy, and different from any of the girls I had previously met. She lived across the street from Greater St. Stephen with her grandmother. I couldn't keep my eyes off of her, even when I was meeting and greeting people after church services. But often, just as quickly as I had seen her, she would disappear into the crowd.

Determined to meet her, I enlisted the aid of one of the ushers to keep track of her for me. Then one day, I caught up with Debra after a service and asked to walk her home. She responded coldly, "No. I live right there. I'm fine." Undaunted, I knew she was the one for me. As far as I was concerned, what I knew was all that mattered.

One Sunday morning, Debra sang in the service. I had no idea she had such talent. She sang the song "When Jesus Comes." She was awesome! That sealed it for me. I had a serious problem, though. Debra was not interested in me.

At the same time, many young women in New Orleans were flirting with me and building up my ego, Debra Brown was avoiding me. There is a warning given in Scripture not to think more highly of yourself than you ought (see Romans 12:3). I struggled with that, because it seemed everyone else was seeking me out and giving me compliments and commendations. I couldn't understand why she wasn't doing the same.

I strategized for the longest time on how I might ask her out and decided the best way was to be direct with her, particularly since my indirect strategies had fallen by the wayside. Seeing her standing alone one day, I said, "Hey, I've been watching you in church and you've probably noticed that I couldn't take my eyes off of you." She responded curtly, "No, I wasn't paying any attention."

Not to be defeated or deflated, I followed up with the classic line: "I was wondering; if you're not busy on Friday night, could I take you out?" She looked at me nonchalantly and said, "No, thanks."

It was as if I was invisible to her. When I persistently asked why she dismissed my friendly overtures, she'd tell me it was none of my business. I was getting little traction with Debra.

It puzzled me how she rejected any possibility of friendship. One day, bristling with indignation, I said: "Everybody in the city is so nice. Why are you so cold?" "I'm not cold," she declared. "I just don't want to go out with you. I'm already going with somebody, and even if I weren't, I don't want to be involved with a preacher. I see how all of the girls are running after you, and I don't play that game."

Then my break came. She continued, "I know you're new in the city, so if you need help getting adjusted, you can call me; but going out with you is out of the question. Furthermore, if you ask me out again, I'll hang up on you!"

This went on for a few months. I just had to tell Debra what I knew in my heart. One day I gathered all the seriousness I could, looked in her eyes, and declared: "God said that you are going to be my wife, so you might as well get with the program!" She became furious. Almost in a state of rage she said, "I have heard many 'lines' from men in my life, but this is the most terrible of all. How dare you use the name of the Lord to move me to date you! I'm certainly not going out with you. Now, God told me that!"

When I thought about it later, I went to her and apologized. I had no idea she would take what I said as being one step short of blasphemy, but I was glad this, at least, gave me an opportunity to speak to her again.

Greater Responsibilities

During this time, Papa Simpson was making full use of my skills and abilities. I was preaching every second Sunday for the youth and every first Sunday night for the Lord's Supper. Then, six months after joining the church, he made me his assistant pastor. The people of Greater St. Stephen were shocked by the announcement, but not nearly as much as I was.

This gave me another great opportunity to approach Debra. I knew that her family had been church founders, and they were all well-respected members of the congregation and community. I decided to use an acknowledgment of her family's history as a way to receive favorable attention from Debra. That strategy backfired.

She became upset with both her mother and me, reiterating that she already had a boyfriend and that neither of us respected the fact that she wasn't interested in me. She later relented and agreed to have dinner with me. That was all I wanted. I made one mistake, though. After bringing her home, I asked for a kiss on the cheek. That was not well received.

Ultimately, my frustration with being rejected by Debra led me to act as if I didn't care, date other girls, and make sure she knew it! It didn't help matters that her relationship with her boyfriend remained "in good standing" the entire time.

As you can tell, I am very persistent when I know God has spoken. My frustration was deeply rooted in the fact that God had said Debra was mine. She was beautiful and eligible—she just wasn't interested in me. At times I wondered if I had heard God clearly. Embracing God's "so that" process concerning Debra was definitely a paradox. God was working out His greater purpose.

Perhaps you've been reminded of some your own paradoxical situations. Keep in mind there's always a reason for every "so that" in your life. Often, God wants us to deal with different areas to expand our thinking and our territory. When we do so, we begin to see who we really are, gain insight from our experiences, and can ultimately help others through their "so that" process.

Now, to avoid confusion, if you are in a situation like mine with the man or woman you believe God has for you, my counsel is simple: Be willing to let that person go. We should fight the "good fight" of faith for what God has spoken until that person marries someone else. When and if that happens, it's time to back off. When God is challenging us to change forward, He never goes against His word.

CHAPTER SEVEN

AN ATMOSPHERE OF JEALOUSY

F rom the beginning of my tenure there, I viewed Greater St. Stephen as a well-organized congregation and was blessed to be part of growing it to the next level. My appointment as assistant pastor, however, had gotten an immediate reaction from others who had served with Papa Simpson for many years. I thank God that we ultimately reconciled.

Because I was new, I was something of a novelty; the congregation applauded much of what I brought to the ministry table. As it happens in many churches, there were those who seemed to be unduly excited about my work, while dismissing the contributions of others who had long labored to make the ministry successful. When the Lord begins to bless, the devil starts a mess!

About six months after coming on staff, things began to change. Papa Simpson began to change toward me, make negative innuendos, and talk about me to others. This was unsettling. Then about a year later (which was two years after I joined the church) he told the congregation: "When I get up, I can hear a pin drop. Our musicians sit at their instruments like bumps on a log, but the moment Paul Morton gets up everybody begins screaming and the musicians go crazy! You can keep that up if you want to, but I will stop him from doing *anything* in this church."

I felt Papa Simpson's words were unjustified. I had been, and would continue to be, loyal to him and to the church. Supporting the man of God had been ingrained in me from childhood.

Not only did I feel blindsided, some of the members were traumatized. Certain people made derogatory comments to me about the pastor, but I wouldn't have it. I had been taught to respect leadership. Some members even remarked they wished I were the pastor, but I quickly dismissed anything that reflected negatively on Papa Simpson. I refused to use my anointing unwisely and give the enemy an opportunity to defame the Lord and our leader. Nevertheless, I was certain jealousy was in the air.

If you are in ministry be careful when people try to "pump you up," especially if it comes at the expense of other leaders. Falling prey to this tactic of the enemy could cause you to miss your destiny. God is not mocked; we reap what we sow (see Galatians 6:7).

Seeking Restoration

It can be difficult to manage relationships when people have hurt you, because it's hard to trust them again. I had never wanted to be the pastor of Greater St. Stephen; I just wanted to help.

I have learned that people can judge your motives to be insincere, especially if you regularly go out of the way to be fair or helpful. Never let the misjudgments of others define you. Be genuine, helpful, sincere, and truthful in everything you do, without hesitation.

These qualities will enable you to serve God and others with excellence. There will always be people who suspect your motives. To change forward you have to keep your eyes on the Lord, and prayerfully do what is pleasing to Him.

Papa Simpson called me later that same night. He said, "Son, I'm sorry. Some of the other pastors in New Orleans were telling me that I should be careful, because you were going to take some of our members away. Frankly, watching how the church had been responding to you I felt a little intimidated, but I know you. You are the most loyal person I've ever met. I know there's something different about you."

We talked for several hours. I did my best to reassure him that I had no interest in Greater St. Stephen beyond my assignment to serve him. I was also assured Papa Simpson loved me deeply; he had just allowed other people to get to him. I was glad we had worked things out.

A Tragic Event

Sadly, tragedy struck only a few days later. Early on Wednesday morning, I received the call that Papa Simpson had been in a fatal accident. I felt as if I could have died right then. Unresolved grief from losing my father at age twelve flooded into my being. Now, at twenty-four years old, I had lost my mentor and father figure.

Papa Simpson had his faults, but as his spiritual son and servant assistant, I felt it was up to me to cover him. Beyond developing and covering me personally, he had opened many doors for me. He placed me on salary as his ministry assistant and helped me to develop relationships with area pastors. Through the church, he had sent me to Union Baptist Theological Seminary where I was furthering my education. Truly, he had blessed my life.

The circumstances of his death only made matters worse. Papa Simpson was driving drunk, accompanied by a woman who wasn't his wife, and they careened over the side of the Lake Pontchartrain Bridge. The lead story on the news that day stated "a big pastor in New Orleans" had died in an auto accident with his mistress.

I knew he had a drinking problem, but felt there was no need to subject him or the congregation to controversy and conflict. It became my task to care for Mama Simpson. She was understandably hurt, grieved, and embarrassed. This kind of ministry challenge was new to me. I loved Papa Simpson dearly, but I had to be there for her as she processed her emotions. Somehow, through God's strength and wisdom, I was able to encourage her to be strong and not allow the devil to get the victory. Then I prepared myself to address our congregation.

As you go about life, unexpected setbacks, disappointments, and even tragedies will come your way. Just don't let them define you. Trust God and remember He's working all things together for your good. The thing that looks like it's about to bring you down is a glorious opportunity to prove God's "so that" process in your life.

CHAPTER EIGHT

STAY IN THE SHIP

The Thanksgiving morning service that was a Greater St. Stephen tradition was taking place in less than twenty-four hours and our senior pastor was deceased. The leadership had to meet. We needed to determine how to handle all the rumors, the emotional uproar, and the uncertainty about the future of the church. We hadn't even had time to plan or hold the funeral.

After deliberating several hours, we decided the Thanksgiving service should go on as planned and that I, as assistant pastor, would conduct it. The members needed to be in one accord. We had to stand strong and do what God wanted us to do.

My challenge was determining what to say to an angry, embarrassed congregation, and I had to start by dealing with my own pain. As I sought the Lord, I asked Him: "What do You want to say to the people?" He opened my understanding. I could see, in the spirit, people jumping ship saying, "I'm outta here!" A word arose in me from Acts 27, which I developed and titled "Stay in the Ship."

In this text the Apostle Paul was on a ship to Rome, where he would be imprisoned. They came into a typhoon that lasted fourteen nights. There was so much panic and confusion even the crew wanted to abandon ship. Acts 27:30-32 (NIV) says: "In an attempt to escape from the ship, the sailors let the lifeboat down into the sea, pretending they were going to lower some anchors from the bow. Then Paul said to the centurion and the soldiers, 'Unless these men stay with the ship, you cannot be saved.' So the soldiers cut the ropes that held the lifeboat and let it fall away."

If the crew had believed the dream Paul told them about several days before, none of them would have tried to escape. Paul had said,

> Men, you should have taken my advice not to sail from Crete; then you would have spared yourselves this damage and loss. But now I urge you to keep up your courage, because not one of you will be lost; only the ship will be destroyed. Last night an angel of the God whose I am and whom I serve stood beside me and said, "Do not be afraid, Paul. You must stand trial before Caesar; and God has graciously given you the lives of all who sail with you." . . . Nevertheless, we must run aground on some island. (vv. 21b-26 NIV)

The untimely death of our pastor had created a climate of unrest at Greater St. Stephen that was threatening to become darker than midnight. Winds of hatred and lies were blowing, but I urged our church family to "stay in the ship." I shared with them that God had given me divine assurance that we would be all right if we didn't try to escape. I encouraged them from Paul's testimony that we could believe God together and overcome. We could trust God to guide us all the way through these troubled waters.

There was a powerful move of God in that service! He had given me the right word, right on time. Members received the message and encouraged each other to "stay in the ship." The devil lost his grip and a great victory was won for the kingdom. People might have been talking about us all over the city, but it became apparent to all that Greater St. Stephen was staying the course.

Navigating Stormy Waters

I was naive to think, however, that our collective victory would be sustained without incident through the completion of Papa Simpson's homegoing service. Due to external influences, and the fact that many of the locals still considered me an outsider, our transition didn't go as smoothly as I would have desired. Against the opposition of Greater St. Stephen, a denominational association put a strategy in place to take over all planning for the funeral and the future direction of the church. I was deliberately excluded from the meetings.

Upon finding out the specifics of their plan, Mama Simpson and the deacons were outraged. They contacted the president of the association and demanded he include me in the funeral program. When you are obediently working through God's "so that" process, you don't have to fight your own battles. He raises up others according to His word who will fight them for you.

The association allowed me to participate only by giving the closing prayer at the cemetery (where fewer people would be in attendance). I knew that I still had God's favor on my life; and I knew victory would ultimately manifest in this situation.

Seeing a New Horizon Line

Immediately after the funeral, the Executive Board of the association met with the deacons and congregation about choosing our next pastor. Their first directive was to leave the pulpit vacant for at least thirty days in honor of the deceased pastor. In the interim, the association would send a different preacher to Greater St. Stephen each week to conduct our service until the church decided which one they wanted.

It seemed apparent the association had already decided on a "preferred candidate," and they made it emphatically clear that my youthfulness disqualified me from being considered. The deacons of Greater St. Stephen took an unusual stand against that tradition. They made it known that I was the congregation's preference to be the next pastor. This process was new to me because of my COGIC background where the Presiding Bishop would "send" the next pastor to the church—and that was that.

Something was up at Greater St. Stephen. There was little argument about leaving the pulpit vacant for thirty days. But a meeting to select the new pastor had been set for December 27, only two days after Christmas! Who would be around to take a church vote then, especially in New Orleans?

Every Sunday and during the week for the next thirty days, visiting preachers came to the church. It was like having a small, never-ending convention. Various ministers arrived, all of them willing to help Greater St. Stephen with whatever we needed; all making themselves available to serve the congregation.

God had allowed me to be at Greater St. Stephen for two years prior to this incident "so that" my heart would be knitted with the hearts of the people. They loved me and I loved them. We had truly become a family. They had seen my loyalty to Papa Simpson and them. They wanted me to be the next pastor.

I called my brother James and told him it appeared the people had chosen me. He cautioned that Baptist church elections don't always go the way they may seem to at first. He knew the denominational procedure of electing a pastor, and didn't want me to be hurt if things didn't go my way. Traditionally, several candidate names were put up for the church vote; afterward, a date was set for the election. The candidate with the most votes won.

James told me setting an election date before the thirty days were ended was uncommon. I was starting to realize, even though we had to walk through the process, God was up to something.

Everything was moving so fast. I felt I needed to let the deacons know how serious I was about the matter. However, as the interim process continued, I began to feel uncomfortable. Many seasoned preachers wanted to pastor at Greater St. Stephen. I decided to be content to remain there and be of help. In fact, during this time while I was talking to the deacons, one of them interrupted me and said, "Rev, shut up. We got this!"

I had to accept a hard truth: I had been taking too much of the burden from the void in our church's leadership upon myself. I had injected myself into the future of that congregation without considering what God had for me.

My brother meant well. He was trying to prepare me for the possibility I wouldn't be selected. I had been relying on what the people were telling me, expecting my future to be based on what they desired. What if God's desire for me was in another place? I was thankful for all the love and favor, but I finally turned my eyes to the Lord and remained prayerful.

Finally, December 27, 1974, arrived. The church was at standing room only. This was exactly thirty days after Papa Simpson's death. They didn't ask me not to attend the meeting, or to leave when the voting took place. My name was the only one considered. I sat silently near the organ. As people entered the church, several made their way through the crowd to let me know they were there for me.

The moderator brought the audience to order. Then Sister Leah Harrell stood and made the motion: "I move that Reverend Paul Morton become the Senior Pastor of Greater St. Stephen Missionary Baptist Church." Immediately, about one hundred people stood to second the motion. Then the chairman called for those in favor to say, "Aye." It was finished.

The congregation erupted, shouting and praising God. Hundreds of people rushed to where I was sitting, each of them hugging and congratulating me. It was a night I'll never forget. This unusual move of God changed my life forever. Now, it was time for us to change forward, overcome our grief, and head into the new horizon.

CHAPTER NINE

RESPECT EARNS RESPECT

As the newly elected pastor of Greater St. Stephen Missionary Baptist Church, I wanted to treat people the way I wanted to be treated and to pastor from a basis of love and respect. Those who are unprepared to lead tend to lord it over people when they get a little power or authority. There is no room for intimidation in spiritual leadership.

As you advance at work or in ministry, it is essential that you honor the position you hold, because if you don't, you may be in for a rude awakening. You must submit to the leadership of the Holy Spirit in everything you do.

I had already had experiences with some "traditional" Baptist thinkers who didn't understand or practice this principle. By saying this, I mean they practiced behaviors that were inappropriate, but had become acceptable in the church. As a result, they often lacked the decorum that honored the Lord and their role in the body of Christ.

As senior pastor, I determined to follow the Holy Spirit. I would be loving but firm. Biblical church discipline had to be a top priority, because character is a key to effective ministry. Too many people have been turned off to church because they encountered gifted believers who lacked spiritual discipline.

Building Accountability

I had grown up under my father's firm leadership and the regimented order of the Pentecostal Church. Therefore, there was a strong ethic of spiritual and personal accountability in our home and congregations. If you did something publicly, you would be subject to rebuke publicly and would be called upon to apologize before the church. In some cases, a leader might have to "sit out" his service for thirty or sixty days or longer, depending on the seriousness of the offense.

In the "traditional" Baptist Church the primary, and often only, offense that required coming before the church was getting behind in paying one's church dues by ninety days or more. In fact, an individual's name could be removed from the church register for that offense. Membership could only be restored by repenting publicly and "begging the church's pardon."

As a people of God, we should embrace accountability "so that" souls can be saved, disciples can be developed, and God's Kingdom can be multiplied. On the local church level, accountability instills "family pride" in church members, loyalty to the pastor, and commitment to the vision of the house. It also ensures the church serves its congregation with excellence.

It's interesting that today's society finds it acceptable to be accountable in every area except in the church. Some pointedly take the position that standards, loyalty, commitment, and order have no place in church life. Think about it. In almost every area of society there are standards of accountability—in business, education, government, and so on. As responsible citizens, we willingly abide by these standards, often without question. How much more should the family of God embrace accountability in His Kingdom?

I was determined to take the church to a new level of discipline. We had in place a threefold invitation after each sermon, including baptism, Christian experience, and watch care. This gave people an opportunity to respond and mature in their spiritual walk.

Breaking Old Paradigms

I learned the big difference between preaching and serving in a pastoral role. A physical fight broke out after one of the church services. As if I were a school principal, somebody came to get me because people were fighting in the parking lot, and they expected me to break it up. I required them to "beg the church's pardon" and dismissed both parties from their appointments for thirty to sixty days.

Soon, I had the reputation that if anyone was brought before me for inappropriate conduct, they would be relieved from any church activities. It was hurtful to some, but I also knew these confrontations were happening because of previous leadership practices. I even noticed subtle reactions during deacon meetings when I raised my voice a little to get my point across.

Papa Simpson had an assertive, even aggressive, personality at times, but was one of the friendliest people you could ever meet. He would frequently stop by the homes of our members, and sit and talk with them for hours. As his spiritual son and assistant, I made some of these visits with him.

Sometimes people would ask, "Rev, do you want something to drink?" His usual response was, "Oh yes! Fix my favorite." I didn't drink wine or alcohol and wasn't used to ministers having a casual drink with church members. Don't get me wrong. I didn't think I was "too good," nor did I think less of him for doing so; I had just seen many times how liquor changed people, and how they could easily lose control. I stayed away from drinking; I was scared of the possible consequences.

A Close Call on the Way to Canada

Sadly, excessive drinking among preachers wasn't unusual at that time. Ephesians 5:18 (KJV) tells us, "And be not drunk with wine, wherein is excess; but be filled with the Spirit." This seemed to imply it was okay for them to drink as long as they didn't overdo it. My experience had been in the Pentecostal church where we opposed drinking altogether and practiced abstinence. We felt it was better to be safe than sorry.

This reminds me of an incident that took place in July 1975 during my first trip back home since becoming pastor of Greater St. Stephen. In the South, people are very friendly and readily embrace "family" relationships in the church. When I traveled to Windsor and Detroit, the church family wanted to go with me. We filled seven busloads and fifty cars for the long journey.

Having left years before—not knowing how or when I'd ever return—this was a major endeavor for me. How would I be received after such a long absence? What would the folks in Windsor and Detroit think about this mass of people who loved their pastor so much, they had followed me over a thousand miles?

I was primarily concerned with the people at home. I soon learned that I should have been more concerned about the folks who were following me on the bus. During our first stop, I learned that some of the "quiet, unassuming" people had gotten high and were revealing their true personalities.

This trip had turned into a motorized Mardi Gras. One "happy" person told me: "Hey, Rev, this is the best trip I've ever been on!" I didn't know how to respond.

Actually, I was a little scared. My Pentecostal roots were deep. I was bringing these people, who were obviously under the influence, to the place where uncompromising ethics had been deeply instilled in me. If even one of those old "Pentecostal church mothers" witnessed this incident, I would have been called into a three-day prayer meeting. I could just hear them saying, "Send him back, Lord! This boy done backslid!" They would have been declaring as a Spirit-filled congregation: "Come out from among them!"

I dispatched two of my deacons and enlisted some family members to take the "offenders" straight to the hotels until they were presentable. Needless to say, I was upset and embarrassed.

However, I have to say that in spite of this wake-up call, I still felt Greater St. Stephen was the greatest church I knew. The people's hearts were pure; they loved me, and I loved them. Yet, I knew that if I were going to present to God the type of church He wanted, I would have to be a serious agent of change.

I could have rationalized to myself that this behavior had been a norm long before I arrived. Who was I to demand change? Would my youthfulness be my downfall if I insisted on their repentance? What would my clergy peers do when they learned how I was taking action in obedience to the Holy Spirit? Would they respond as I did to the Lord's challenge for greater pastoral accountability?

Leaders often find themselves in these types of paradoxical situations. On the one hand, we want to be understanding and continue to be well-liked. On the other hand, we have to stand firm in our God-given assignment as responsible stewards. I knew at that moment, in order to fully claim the mantle of leadership for which I had been ordained, I would have to be willing to take unpopular stands. I would have to lead our church into an unsettling process "so that" we could become all He intended us to be. This situation represented the turning point for our congregation.

CHAPTER TEN

STRIVING FOR EXCELLENCE

It was definitely time to change forward. Upon returning to New Orleans I called everyone together and introduced our new church theme: "Striving for Excellence." I challenged them that we had to dare to be different from other Baptist churches. We were part of a "chosen generation." We were going to learn how to do well and embrace excellence in every area of our lives.

Again, my more structured background helped me. My father had been a disciplined man. Besides pastoring "one church in two locations" and birthing other new churches, he had a thirty-minute broadcast, initially called "The Dawn Patrol," which was broadcast on a 50,000-watt station that covered much of the East coast. Everything we did had to be precise and timely.

rom this foundation, the Lord helped me to begin reshaping Greater St. Stephen. God was calling us to be a serious people who diligently advanced His Kingdom.

The process began. If someone was doing something the wrong way in the office, we would quickly correct them so it could be "done well." There were times we had to remind singers not to give a speech before their solo. We expected Sunday school teachers to be disciplined, to study diligently for class and get enough rest the night before. We focused on enhancing every area. It was hard at first, especially since I was a young pastor, but I firmly believed in excellence

"Striving for Excellence" became my heart's cry to the congregation. I kept reinforcing it, because faith comes by hearing, according to the word of God (see Romans 10:17).

Confronting a Major Stronghold

Giving, of course, was of primary importance to maintaining church operations. Beyond this, we needed to reach out to the community in greater ways. If we were going to go to the next level, our old system had to change.

My first assignment was to break the stronghold in people's minds that church dues were supposed to be our primary means of support. It was important to replace that mindset by teaching them biblical giving through tithes and offerings. Up to that point, each member had been accustomed to paying dues of at least two dollars weekly, and they did it faithfully. They had done so for years. Greater St. Stephen had 647 dues-paying members, and though a few paid more, two-dollar weekly contributions were the norm.

Our annual "Women's Day" event had brought in the most money. The church budget at that time was about $59,000. "Women's Day" brought in $36,000 using a fundraising method called "keys and locks." Much of this plan's success was attributed to Sister Leah Harrell. She was a strong, influential leader. She was the person who had stood and made the motion for the church to vote me in as pastor. When Sister Harrell spoke, everyone listened. We needed to start doing things God's way. One day I called Sister Harrell into my office to discuss making this change. She wasn't receptive to changing forward. In fact, she flat out told me that no one in our church was going to give 10 percent of his or her income.

God reminded me that any changes I orchestrated would be the result of winning the hearts of the people. So, I kept teaching, preaching, and reinforcing excellence, preparing the hearts of the people.

Implementing Change

I waited until the fall of 1976 (about a year after our meeting) to take definitive action. For now, we were in the midst of unsettling transitions, so my primary focus was on my pastoral responsibilities. I had to decide once and for all, the direction our church was going to take. With some trepidation, I called a church meeting after a Sunday worship service. It was time to settle things and start doing things God's way, not the old way of paying dues and depending on one annual event to tide us over. We had to embrace change and operate according to His principles.

Some members proclaimed the virtues of Sister Harrell: how the church wouldn't be where it was if it hadn't been for her. I was just trying to help them understand that my goal wasn't to displace her. We simply were no longer going to operate God's church primarily from "keys and locks" income and chicken dinners. It was time for us to believe God and stretch our faith "so that" Greater St. Stephen could flourish and have the impact He intended.

The Spirit directed me to call for a vote on whether the church would follow the Bible or continue in its old ways. The congregation overwhelmingly stood with me. I was happy to have gained everyone's support, yet I have to admit it was one of my most trying days as pastor.

I wanted everybody to work in unity. For several months after that meeting, Sister Harrell and three other women showed up every Sunday, sat on the same pew, and turned their faces the opposite way while I preached. God wouldn't permit me to say anything to them or to preach about it. Ultimately, their behavior changed and things started turning for the better.

Divine Multiplication

I was in awe as I witnessed what God was doing at Greater St. Stephen. During my first year as pastor we took in more new members than we had total during my first two years at the church. By His Spirit, God added over 1,200 new members! We had to turn people away every Sunday while others were still standing outside. One day someone told me we had turned away more than 150 people.

I knew we couldn't grow the kingdom by sending people away. At that time, churches weren't holding multiple services; we didn't have a model for that. So, it was time to expand. We started our building fund in 1977.

The only way to change forward is to do things God's way—even when it hurts. I knew God had called our church to move forward and do more for His Kingdom. I pray, like me, you'll receive the grace to see beyond every challenge and *change forward*. When you do, you'll experience God's unlimited power in your life.

CHAPTER ELEVEN

MANIFOLD TRIALS: STUMBLING BLOCKS OR STEPPING STONES

B uilding a new facility in Uptown New Orleans was difficult because the church was land-locked on South Liberty Street. There was a bar to our left and property with an absentee owner on the right. Initially, the owner of the bar didn't want to sell the property, but we prayed until customers stopped coming. It eventually closed, and we happily bought the property in 1978, but we still needed the property on the other side of the church if we were going to build.

The owner of the property on the right, whom I will call Mrs. Jones, lived about a half block away. For some reason, she hated Papa Simpson. When he passed and I became Senior Pastor, she seemed determined to take it out on me. My prayers and attempts to persuade her were of no effect. She was immovable. Whenever I approached her about selling her property to us, it was like hitting a brick wall. I asked the church to continue in prayer that she would change her mind.

Greater St. Stephen was located in a rough part of the city, but the gangsters there loved me. If someone approached me who seemed to be a problem, one of them would come over to make sure everything was all right. I thank God for favor. It's a blessing when even the world respects you. I later found out the reason the church had never been vandalized was that word had been put out on the street: Greater St. Stephen and its preacher were off limits.

One day while we were in the process of approaching Mrs. Jones, one of the gangsters heard about it and came by to tell me if we really wanted it, all I had to do was give him the word. The house would be gone the next day. He was going to burn it down for us. I immediately said, "Lord, no!" I had to convince him to let God work it out.

I went repeatedly to see Mrs. Jones who was about seventy years old. Determined not to sell her property to us, she warned me not to raise the issue again when and if I came to her house.

That was fine with me, because God had already told me to stop talking to her about it, and to just go visit her from time to time. When I went to see her I could tell that she wasn't used to having many visitors. As time passed, she even started looking forward to my visits, but I never mentioned the house.

Then one day while I was visiting, she asked me point blank: "You want that house, don't you?" Somewhat nonchalantly, I said, "What house?" She looked at me sternly and said, "Don't play with me, boy! You want that house, don't you? Say 'I want it!' " I was stunned into silence. Then she smiled at me and said, "It's yours. Have your people get with mine, and we'll draw up the papers."

Patience is a virtue; it's a vital part of changing forward. Not only did she change her mind: the Lord allowed us to develop a beautiful relationship.

Growing Pains

The church was steadily growing. But some of the local pastors resented our growth; they felt it had come at their expense. Whenever our church hit a new benchmark of progress, a spirit of resentment surfaced.

I didn't pastor in isolation from the community. I was involved in a number of political events, including the election of New Orleans' first Black mayor, Ernest N. Morial. The participation of area churches turned out to be an important factor, and people felt a deep sense of civic pride when he was elected. Then the dialogue started—if you wanted to be elected to a public office, you had to "talk with Paul Morton." I had to admit this was partially true, but I was happy when they added, "but he can't be bought."

There was an attempt to close a local gospel radio station. It was the only outlet for African-American churches and pastors to reach larger audiences. I led the march on the station. This was a radical move, and we saved the station.

I took the position that if I was going to be slandered or demeaned, it would be the result of my doing good. As the church grew in numbers and influence, there were some who really loved me and others who really hated me. I had to learn how to live with that. It's not always the case that others automatically seek out and celebrate the good in you.

God Proves Our Faith "So That" We Thrive

I was learning some difficult, yet important, life lessons. 1 Peter 1:6-7 states: "Wherein ye greatly rejoice [because of being kept by the power of God through faith], though now for a season, if need be, ye are in heaviness through manifold temptations. That the trial of your faith, being much more precious than of gold that perisheth, though it be tried with fire, might be found unto praise and honor and glory at the appearing of Jesus Christ" (KJV).

We don't hear much in twenty-first-century America about being severely persecuted or killed for the sake of the gospel. The Apostle Paul ended up going to Nero's chopping block and dying for the sake of the Lord. Yet, he was still able to say: "I am now ready to be offered, and the time of my departure is at hand. I have fought a good fight, I have finished my course, I have kept the faith" (2 Timothy 4:6-7, KJV). Neither do we hear stories about people who, like Stephen, have been put to death for having vibrant faith in the Lord. (See Acts 6:8–7:60.)

Things aren't that bad for us. But there comes a time in every Christian's life when one's faith is put to the test. The Bible calls these tests "manifold temptations" and "trials of our faith."

Other trials may come because of your loyalty and commitment to truth. Some people don't want to be convicted about their sins. They prefer to skip over things like adultery, fornication, same-sex marriage, common law situations, and so on. They want the preacher to stay out of their personal business because it might require them to face the truth and change forward.

Why does God allow manifold trials to come in our lives? According to 1 Peter 1:6-7, they prove our faith. Your faith is *proven* when it is *revealed to others*. God wants to reveal and emphasize your faith. He does so by letting "clouds" (problems) come into your life "so that" the loveliness of the sun, moon, and stars can be revealed. It is when "clouds" appear that the beauty of your faith shines forth. Otherwise, it would be commonplace, ordinary.

Manifold trials strengthen and confirm faith. Think of it this way. Trees need every season to become strong. Adverse winds and pounding rains "try" and invigorate them. If a tree were to have sunshine all the time it would dry out. If it had rain all the time, it would "flood out." Trees need the balance of weathering every season. All things work together for good.

Palm trees were planted in my yard. I loved those trees. I looked at them as sponsoring a little taste of Hawaii in New Orleans. In 1989, however, we had the coldest winter ever. Those palm trees died, but across the street, there was an oak tree still standing. No matter how cold it got, that tree stood in the place it had stood for years. If that oak tree had a voice it might have said, "I can handle this cold New Orleans. I have some cousin oak trees in Detroit, New York, Canada. I can handle it because, unlike the palm trees, I can handle all of the seasons."

In a personal way, part of my life resembles this story. When I moved to New Orleans, I must confess that I was a "palm tree." I was the "baby Paul" in my family, whom everybody loved because he was "just like his daddy." I had the protection and support of the family's love, but when I relocated to New Orleans and established a fast-growing church, people started lying and slandering my name. I wasn't accustomed to that kind of reception or treatment and I would, sometimes, go to my room and cry over it. All I wanted to do was help people and I wasn't used to the envy and jealousy among local preachers.

My enemies were determined to flood the city with rumors and innuendoes, but they made the mistake of continuing to talk about me; and the more they talked, the more I bowed on my knees. I spent time talking to God and never complaining to anyone else. It turned me from a "palm tree" to an "oak tree." God will allow some things to happen in your life to make you stronger. You have to remember that it's only a test.

I praise the Lord for His "so that" process, because the more people talked about me, the more I went to God for strength. During those first "inclement" years, I learned to spend time talking to God and never complaining to anyone else. I encourage you to let God acclimate your faith, so you thrive when times are tough. The things He allows to happen in your life will make you stronger if you keep your eyes on Him.

CHAPTER TWELVE

THE NEED
FOR BALANCE

A t the same time that God was growing Greater St. Stephen, He was still telling me that He had a wife and a life partner for me. God had already shown me Debra. For the next couple of years, I befriended her to the point that she felt she could talk to me about anything. But I wanted to be more than her friend.

Debra called me after Papa Simpson died. She knew we had been very close and was right there for me during that extremely difficult time. I will admit I may have taken advantage of her sympathy to get her attention.

That Christmas I splurged and bought her an eighteen-inch television. Though I would soon become pastor, I was still earning seventy-five dollars a week. That TV took everything I had. Then she had the nerve to tell me she couldn't accept the gift because her boyfriend might get upset!

By now, I was in good standing with Debra's family. She lived with her grandmother, to whom I told how Debra had rejected a perfectly good television because of her boyfriend. Debra's grandmother pulled Debra aside and told her she shouldn't hurt my feelings and that she should accept my gift. (Actually, I think Debra really wanted the television anyway; she just needed an excuse to tell her boyfriend.) She loved that television and ended up keeping it long after we were married.

Before I became Senior Pastor I was able to afford a 1968 Malibu convertible to replace the 1959 Buick I had been driving. Receiving numerous preaching engagements each week, I was soon able to afford a 1973 Grand Prix. This was my first new car and I loved it. One day, I invited Debra to take my car and go out with her girlfriends. I could see in her eyes how excited she was. She took the keys and took off with two of her friends. I knew I was getting to her.

A Sudden Change of Heart

Finally, she broke off her relationship with her boyfriend. So I asked her to go for a drive down to the lake. My invitation definitely wasn't well received. You would have thought I had invited her to share a room with me at a local motel. Her reaction was "vintage Debra": "Men only have one thing on their minds!" But she was finally willing to be my girlfriend.

Debra often told me that I acted "too old." She was right. I definitely had a tendency to act older than my age. I wore a suit every day, even to church picnics. To me, maintaining my public image was important. Debra brought a needed balance into my life. Though I was the "Reverend," she could bring out the "Paul" in me. She could make me laugh like no one else.

I had a few scary moments with her father. He made it clear to me that I had better not do any harm to his daughter. Mr. Brown always reminded me how good Debra was and that she deserved a strong—not abusive—man.

Realizing the Dream

Although I was already functioning as Senior Pastor, I was determined to complete my studies. It was difficult, but in May 1975, I was able to graduate from Union Baptist Theological Seminary with honors. With that in place, I was ready to settle down in marriage. I had turned twenty-five and Debra was twenty-one, and in her last year of college.

No matter how much I talked about getting married, Debra kept emphasizing she had to finish her degree. I tried to convince her that my salary was sufficient to support us. I was probably the highest paid pastor in New Orleans at that time. This carried no weight with Debra. She made it clear when she got her degree in Communications, *she* would make more than I did. That didn't sit very well with me, but I loved her deeply and resolved to support her wishes.

Around the same time, the deacons at Greater St. Stephen approached me about getting married and we had our first, and only, major disagreement. They said, "Reverend, we think you ought to settle down. We think you need a wife!" The church was growing and, because I was single, they were having issues with some of the young women who seemed to be attracted to me.

I don't think the deacons were prepared for my reaction. I was furious. I let them know that no one was going to *force* me into marriage. They quickly clarified that they weren't insisting I marry: they were only letting me know "some of the members were concerned." My "flesh" took over. I couldn't resist snapping, "If you don't like it, you can take this old church back! I'm not going to be rushed into marriage!"

In a way, though, they had confirmed my feelings; maybe that's why I reacted. When I calmed down, I knew they meant well. The fact was *I* wanted to be married more than *they* wanted me to be married—but Debra felt she was "too young." She wanted to finish college first. I had to trust God and honor her desires.

Not long after, I took Debra to a five-star restaurant called Masson's and asked for her hand in marriage. That became the most exciting day of my life *because she said yes!* A year later, on December 18, 1976, we were married. I was ecstatic then, and am even happier now, because Debra B. Morton has made my life complete.

Our wedding was such a major event in New Orleans that many people couldn't get in the church. God blessed our union, because she conceived our first child, Jasmine, on our honeymoon. We had everything planned—except that! So, Debra put her last year of college on hold. Her top priority would soon be staying at home with our new baby girl. Jasmine was born in September 1977.

To this day, I commend Debra for her faithfulness and dedication. When we got married, not only did we have a growing church, but I was becoming a popular evangelist. There were many weeks I was gone, though I tried to stay home as much as possible.

Added to this, Debra was a young "first lady," which made some other women jealous. Debra was so strong. She knew how to handle people with love. She was wise beyond her years and actively involved in the ministry.

The people of Greater St. Stephen learned to love and embrace her. I had never wanted my wife to be the typical first lady. I needed a down-to-earth woman who would make me laugh and challenge me to be the best I could be. I thank God for giving me Debra. When we became one, He blessed our family and ministry beyond measure. Debra and I quickly learned how to grow with the changes. God was doing incredible things in our lives and at Greater St. Stephen.

CHAPTER THIRTEEN

RECKLESS
FAITH

Many times when walking through God's "so that" process your faith can seem reckless to others. This is part of the paradox of changing forward. As the Lord expanded our territory at Greater St. Stephen we often had to see and take action beyond our natural thoughts and abilities. Before we knew it, we were moving into our new 1,500-seat facility in January 1980. Immediately, the church was packed every Sunday.

During that dynamic time, our church choir had completed its first recording on our in-house label: a remake of Reverend James Cleveland's song, "The Sun Will Shine After Awhile." A few years later, because of the many industry contacts the Lord blessed us to develop, we went with a national record label.

God also told me to start a television broadcast, so I announced it to the church but forgot to mention it to the deacons first. With the greatest of respect for them, I sought their forgiveness. I explained that when I announced God had told us to do this, I didn't think anyone would assume we needed to vote on His decision. They all understood and said "Amen." This was a new season for our ministry; not everything needed to be put to a vote. Our program, "Changing a Generation," soon became the most popular Saturday morning broadcast. Thousands of lives were changed because we listened to the voice of God.

At the same time, God was adding to the Morton family. Debra and I had our second child—a son—in 1981. We named him Paul Jr.

God had also been working out the process with Sister Harrell. She saw how, through biblical tithing, we were able to grow the ministry, build a new facility, and expand our outreaches. However, she became very ill the year Paul was born. One day she called me to her bedside at the hospital. She reached for my hand and said, "I never told you this, but you're doing a great job. Thank you for taking the stand that you did. Always listen to God and not people, no matter how powerful they may be—including me."

We both laughed, and then she asked me to forgive her. I thank God we reconciled; I had always wanted that. Then in 1982, God called her home. I was glad the Lord allowed her to live long enough to see and take part in expanding the ministry from where we were in 1976. Sister Harrell might have been elderly, but she didn't let it stop her from changing forward.

Walking on Water

God always tells me to do something new when the budget is tight. When advancing the Kingdom of God, there are definitely times when we have to step out of our comfort zones in faith and "walk on the water" to Jesus.

Matthew 14:22-33, is the amazing story of Jesus, as He walks on the water during a violent storm. But when Peter heard the Lord's voice, he asked Jesus to call him out on the water (vv. 26-28).

The devil can smell fear. He wages warfare against us, trying to distract us with stormy circumstances so we'll give in to our fear, instead of hearing the voice of God.

As long as we're in human flesh, Jesus keeps calling us out of the "boat" to rise to new and higher ways of living. That's what Peter did. Some people call this reckless; I call it reckless faith.

Jesus came in human form "so that" we could become like Him. No matter what we face, we are built to rise above it. I encourage you to seek God, meditate on His Word, and tune your spiritual ears to hear His voice *before storms come*. When you keep communication lines open with Jesus before the storm, you'll be able to recognize His voice during the storm.

God was taking Greater St. Stephen to another level, and teaching the people about faith. When it comes to the spiritual things of God, we have to understand it's not a "mind thing." We simply need to trust God and do what He tells us to do.

Renowned preacher, Charles Spurgeon once said: " 'I will do as much as I can' says one. Any fool can do that. He that believes in Christ does what he cannot do: attempts the impossible and performs it."[1] Legendary civil rights leader, Dr. Martin Luther King, Jr., delivered many powerful messages. One of the things he said in his last speech that affected me greatly was, "it really doesn't matter to me now, because I've been to the mountaintop."[2] Dr. King was saying that he knew his assignment and no matter what happened, he was going to change forward. It no longer mattered how long he lived or if people opposed him. He just wanted to do God's will.

Let me make a final point about walking on the water with Jesus. Hearing the voice of the Lord was enough for Peter to take that first big step of faith. He had a bold, obedient mindset. No doubt, the other disciples probably wanted to shout: "Peter, you have zeal, but it's not according to knowledge. You're not Jesus!" They didn't grasp the only thing he needed at that moment was a word from the Lord.

I have learned in order to be a "water walker" and to deal effectively with seemingly impossible situations, one of the first things I need to do is separate myself from negative people. Don't let anything or anyone keep you from pursuing your God-given destiny.

Be like Peter. As the story goes, though, Peter looked around while walking to Jesus on the water and started to sink—but the Lord caught him (see Matthew 14:30-31). If Peter had kept his eyes on Jesus, he could have made it all the way without going under.

When I heard the voice of the Lord and excitedly told the church we would be starting a television ministry, I was stepping out of the boat in the midst of dynamic change! I truly believe that was another turning point for our church. I had the integrity of always seeking the Lord's favor and Word. Some of the deacons hadn't been accustomed to this style of leadership. I told them I would always let them know when I had heard the Lord, or when I was doing something I wanted to do. Let me encourage you that you can do all things through Christ who strengthens you! As you change forward and God continues to multiply His blessing in your life, you'll have to deal with the challenges associated with expansion and growth. This is all part of His "so that" process. To keep changing forward, Jesus requires you to have great faith, reckless faith, in Him.

CHAPTER FOURTEEN

DEVELOPING TEAM EXCELLENCE

———

I knew that if Greater St. Stephen was going to be successful it had to be a team effort. I had seen so many pastors, including my father, try to do too much alone. With the explosive growth, we were on the way to becoming a megachurch, even though the word or model did not yet exist at that time. We had to depend on the wisdom and grace of God.

Ephesians 4:11-12 tells us the Lord gave fivefold ministry gifts, including the pastoral office, "for the equipping of the saints for the work of ministry." At the time, our church staff consisted of a secretary, a janitor and two musicians (only one musician was being paid). Now it was clearly time to move to the next level. It would take a team of ministers to meet the people's needs with excellence

I needed to add staff who shared my heart and vision for ministry. The first position I created was a Pastor of Healing and Visitation, which was a blessing, but a challenge, too, as some people only wanted me to visit them.

We determined that we needed to add a minister of music, a drummer, and a guitarist. This was a hard change for many but we were called to embrace excellence and that meant paying musicians for their work. Our worship band became an extraordinary example for the glory of God.

We also needed more people in the finance office. Church giving had tripled, which increased our responsibility to be financially accountable. We had to add staff to be prepared for what God was going to release to us.

The need for pastoral counseling also increased significantly. We took the needed steps to change forward.

By 1985 we were turning people away again because we'd maximized our space. In the old church we could seat about five hundred worshippers and now we could seat two thousand. I was thankful for the favor, but I also knew if people couldn't get into the building, they'd find another church.

It was time for multiple services. We established two Sunday services at eight a.m. and eleven a.m. This immediately absorbed the increased growth.

I've always developed people toward excellence, because again, many people "do church," but without a sense of order and timing. As God's people, we shouldn't let His house become a place where "anything goes." This insults His very presence. Everything we do should reflect the excellence of God.

Proverbs 29:18 (KJV) tells us that without a vision the people perish. So, we established a sixteen-step vision for our church and appointed an administrator who specialized in that area. We began holding an orientation class for new members, so they could be clear about our vision. Other ministries started approaching us to learn more about what we were doing.

Learning to "Do Well"

I base my paradigm of developing people on one of my favorite scriptures, Isaiah 1:17a (KJV), which simply says: "Learn to do well."

Human beings are best defined by our ability to learn. Here's how I break down the process:

> **Learn**—you need to focus on searching for, discovering, getting, hearing, seeing, and mastering what God has for you.
>
> **To Do**—you need to posture yourself to achieve and complete, not start and stop. You can't get to "well" until you learn TO DO! To "do" you need to listen to, *and* follow, sound instruction. You need to have a humble, diligent mindset.
>
> **Well**—you must focus on doing things correctly and in an acceptable manner. To me, "half done" is never acceptable.

Over the years I have developed the "three P's" of doing well. *The first "P" stands for "Pattern."* The first step in doing well is to learn according to God's pattern in His Word and through your spiritual leadership. You need a role model to follow. Jesus is our ultimate example.

The second "P" stands for "Power." I'm talking about the power of the Holy Ghost. I've worked diligently to teach God's people we're not created to do things in our own power. We can only "do well" for God by letting the Holy Spirit reign over our minds.

The third "P" stands for "Practice." The correct way "to do" God's work is to keep doing it until you get it right. Discipline can be boring, because it requires you to keep doing something until you master it. I preach it, teach it, walk it, and talk it. As you trust God, He'll give you everything you need to face and rise above every challenge.

One Church in Two Locations

In 1986, God told me to prepare to expand our territory. I knew that we couldn't move the old landmark church. It was the "mother church" and our people felt it was on sacred ground. However, we were literally boxed in. The City of New Orleans is divided into three major sections: Uptown, East, and West Bank. God told me to look at East New Orleans.

Almost two years later, with great help from my wife, we found Word of Faith Church. It was just what we needed, with seating for about eight hundred people. Now, we had to decide how to tell our congregation what God had told us to do. We knew many of them had never heard of "one church in two locations."

Of course, I was comfortable with this concept because I had learned from my father's experience. As I shared the vision, I told the congregation there was an area of New Orleans that wasn't being served and used the McDonald's example of "there's one near you."

Our people caught the vision and we moved forward raising money for our second location.

God gave me a plan that I called the "extra-milers." Since the East location could seat eight hundred at that time, I asked four hundred members to commit to worshiping there for six months. We didn't discriminate on who could decide to go—and that included deacons, ushers, choir members, and so on. After the six months, they had the option to return to our Uptown location.

The concept worked as God had promised. When we held the East location's dedication service in May 1992, after tearing down the old building and replacing it with one that seated three thousand, the church was filled to capacity. The following Sunday, we preached at eight a.m. in the East location, and then held services at ten a.m. and noon at the Uptown location. Word spread quickly about "one church in two locations" and, once again, the membership increased.

We were compelled to continue to expand.. There was a separate building on the grounds of the East location that had been a gymnasium; we worshipped there while we were expanding. We named that space, which seated about one thousand worshipers, A. A. Gundy Hall, after the founding pastor of Greater St. Stephen.

I was still conducting week-long revivals and coming home on the weekends. Preaching became a difficult balancing act. Over time, God had raised my pastoral salary quite a bit from the original $250 a week, but I had to preach outside of Greater St. Stephen to make ends meet. We were now a family of five: Jasmine, Paul Jr., and our beautiful daughter Christiann was about a year old.

The Blessing of Obedience

It wasn't long before I was shown favor at National Baptist Convention. They had Late Night Service at the annual events, where lesser-known preachers were allowed to preach before some of the best preachers in the country. I was invited to preach at one of those late services.

When Dr. T. J. Jemison (from Louisiana) became president, opportunities for me became greater. He allowed me to preach in the "parent body" of the convention, as well as in the National Sunday School and B.T.U. Congress.

Being affiliated with the convention resulted in a number of invitations to do revivals that kept me traveling up to thirty weeks of the year. God told me I had to slow down and give more time to my family and to weekly Bible studies. The people needed to be taught, and it was my responsibility to do it. When I came off the road, hundreds of people began attending weekly Bible study, and we changed its name to Word Explosion.

CHAPTER FIFTEEN

THE EMPOWERMENT OF THE HOLY GHOST

A nother dynamic event was taking place in the spiritual realm during our expansion. One day in 1990 I heard in my spirit: though we had many members, what was the value of having a large church with no power?

I couldn't deny what God was revealing to my spirit: It was time to bring our church, and all Baptist churches for that matter, into the fullness of the Holy Ghost. People had been taught about the triune nature of God: Father, Son, and Holy Ghost, but they didn't understand the power of the Holy Ghost.

As believers, they needed to know who the Father had sent to "guide us into all truth" after Jesus ascended to heaven (see John 16:13 and Acts 1:4-9). They needed to understand that Jesus said "signs" would follow those who believe. By the power of the Holy Ghost they could cast out demons, lay hands on the sick and see them recover, and among other things, speak with new tongues (see Mark 16:17-18).

I would do exactly what the Spirit told me to do. The devil didn't want that. He sent a threatening thought: "you're going to lose all your members." I took a stand on faith. The Spirit guided me as I taught our people. It would take me more than two years to get the church to the place where we could operate in what I had been teaching.

Around that same time my wife took a group of ladies from our ministry to a women's conference at Dr. Fredrick K. C. Price's church in California. They returned filled with the Holy Ghost! These bold women were among the first to experience the dynamic change that was coming to the entire congregation. There was no denying it—the pressure to change was building, but God confirmed to my spirit that He'd let me know when the time was right.

Finally, the day arrived. I declared: "It's time to receive the baptism of the Holy Ghost!" The response was unlike anything I'd ever seen. Hundreds of people came to the altar and were filled with the Holy Ghost, all of them demonstrating the "evidence" of speaking in tongues.

Now, let me clarify. Speaking in tongues isn't the *qualifier*, but an *indicator*, that a person has received this "baptism." Speaking in tongues can be compared to wearing a wedding ring. A ring doesn't *qualify* that a person is married; some people wear a wedding ring to avoid being pursued romantically. The Bible clearly says speaking with "new tongues" is one of the "signs" that would follow those who believe.

Transition Pains

We were expanding to East New Orleans at the same time we were expanding in the realm of the Spirit. The Baptist Church has a strong foundation, because we focus on getting people saved. The Pentecostal Church focuses more on people receiving the Holy Ghost with evidence of speaking in tongues. Putting them together was the perfect marriage: salvation first, then the baptism of the Holy Ghost—resulting in the "fullest" experience with God in this world.

I have to say, however, we weren't the first church in New Orleans to make this transition. God started the process in our city by using a good friend of mine, Prophet Robert Charles Blakes. He had an encounter with God, got filled with the Holy Ghost, and became a totally different person. After that, his church, New Home, made the transition to embrace the "full" Christian experience.

Usually when a Baptist church makes this kind of transition, it drops the name "Baptist." God didn't tell me to do that. Obviously, the easiest way to maintain relationship with the Pentecostal church would have been to call ourselves "Full Gospel." That way, the people with that background would have seen me as having stayed with my roots. The Baptists, on the other hand, would have felt that by dropping the name "Baptist," we had left the Baptist church. God told me to call Greater St. Stephen a "Full Gospel Baptist" church.

In 1992, the same year we completed the East location, we changed our church name from "Greater St. Stephen Missionary Baptist Church" to "Greater St. Stephen Full Gospel Baptist Church." This new name clearly identified who we were becoming. I also changed my title from "Reverend Paul Morton" to "Elder Paul Morton."

There was intense spiritual warfare. Though God had confirmed our transition with "much fruit" after my big church announcement, many people still had a ways to go in His "so that" process. Many people, on both sides, felt that a harmful schism would come in the church if I continued on my trek to usher in the power of the Holy Ghost.

Of course, the "harmful schism" never happened. God did the opposite in our ministry. Greater St. Stephen ended up doubling in growth, even to the point that Baptists, Pentecostals, and nondenominationalists wanted to join the church. I thank God for giving His wisdom and power to bring us all the way through the process "so that" we could be an effective witness to many.

Having gone to a new level in the Spirit, we began to give a five-fold invitation after each message: (1) to accept Jesus Christ as Savior and Lord; (2) to join the church by Christian experience; (3) to return to Christ if one has backslidden; (4) to be filled with the Holy Ghost; and (5) to come under "watch care" if someone is in our city for work or school, but their church is still back home. Although transition is usually awkward (sometimes even painful) at first, God always confirms His direction with supernatural results.

A "New Day" in the Spirit

During this season, churches were rapidly dropping denominational designations, but I knew God had shown me that my assignment was to bring the two largest denominations (Baptist and Pentecostals) together. This concept would enable other Baptist pastors who had been filled with the Holy Ghost to transition their churches without leaving the Baptist church.

In September 1992 I was invited to preach at the National Baptist Convention. The moderator introduced me as "the pastor of the fastest growing church in the convention." He also said: "He calls himself 'Elder Paul Morton' now and the name of the church that he pastors is 'Greater St. Stephen Full Gospel Baptist Church' " He laughed and continued, and the audience responded in laugher. After this introduction, I knew what God had called me to do.

I had enjoyed the fellowship and I wanted to stay in the convention as a "Pentecostal Baptist." As long as it was just me, that wasn't a problem. The convention leadership probably dismissed me as being a young, zealous preacher. Neither they nor I knew what God was about to do.

I had preached at the convention many times before I had begun our church's transition, but the anointing was heavily upon me this day. God had given me a word from Isaiah 2:2-4, which I titled "A Transformed World." I did not know as I prepared the message that it would be a declaration of God's intent for His people. This passage reads:

> Now it shall come to pass in the latter days that the mountain of the Lord's house shall be established on the top of the mountains, and shall be exalted above the hills; and all nations shall flow to it. Many people shall come and say, "Come, and let us go up to the mountain of the Lord, to the house of the God of Jacob; He will teach us His ways, and we will walk in His paths." For out of Zion shall go forth the law, and the word of the Lord from Jerusalem. He shall judge between the nations, and rebuke many people; they shall beat their swords into plowshares, and their spears into pruning hooks; nation shall not lift up sword against nation, neither shall they learn war anymore.

As I preached, I began to prophesy that a "new day" was about to take place. A transforming change was about to take place; the Holy Spirit was declaring through me that it was about to happen. Even at that moment, transformation was in the air.

The response from the audience was so great that they couldn't restore order. People all over the building were praising God. The moderator of the convention was hitting his gavel on the table as hard as he could, screaming: "Order, Order, Order! We must have order!" God was moving. Nobody could stop it.

I was soaking wet from perspiration, so they ushered me into a little room behind the stage to change clothes. While I was still undressing the president of the convention burst into the room and startled me. As I tried frantically to cover my nakedness, he said, "Paul, you've got something like I've never seen before. These people love you. Listen to them. They can't stop them. When you preach . . ." (he was searching for a word to describe what he thought had happened) "You've got 'presence.' " I said, "No, Mr. President; it's called 'the anointing!'" He paused, and then looked directly at me and said, "Call it whatever you want. You've got it!"

I didn't know that would be the last time I preached at the convention. As I left the meeting hall, my dear friend, Dr. Norman Owens, lifted up my hands like a winning prizefighter and said, "Be our Bishop. Be our Bishop." To him, using the word "Bishop" was a joke (because I had changed my title to Elder), but at the same time, his words were highly prophetic. God was in the process of moving me out of the convention.

There can be no greater example of spiritual warfare than that which took place after that night. My spirit was in warfare with my mind, and my mind was at war with the Spirit. I knew the president of the convention didn't want to lose me or Greater St. Stephen; not only did we have a great relationship, the church was one of its largest financial supporters. We were both "Louisiana boys" and he had never hidden the fact that he had designs for me in the convention.

God was clearly telling me that I had to get out. I especially didn't want to part with my best friend, Dr. Moses Gordon, because he was my traveling partner. I hadn't planned to leave the National Baptist Convention, but the Holy Ghost was guiding me to move forward.

I received confirmation that year at the Late Night Service, when a leading speaker, from the stage, mocked the Holy Spirit and even specifically mocked one of my dearest colleagues who was present in the hall. It was confirmed for me when Debra leaned over to me and said, "I've got to get out of here!" I said, "Can't you wait until the lecturer is finished?" "No!" she exclaimed. I left with her.

I had to ask myself why I had remained in the convention so long after God had spoken to me. His words were still resonating in my spirit: "Do you think I have blessed Greater St. Stephen like I have, and transitioned it into a greater church, for you to keep this to yourself? No! What has happened at Greater St. Stephen is going to happen all over the world."

Listen carefully. Always remain sensitive to the voice of the Lord, because every season has a beginning and an end. We are often tempted to remain in places where God has blessed us in the past. But when He tells us to move, we need to trust Him and go. Changing forward means letting go of what we know—no matter how good or bad it may be—to lay hold of a future only God can show us.

CHAPTER SIXTEEN

GOD'S MOVEMENT

In every way I could imagine 1992 and 1993 were years of dynamic change. The momentum was accelerating. We had already transitioned in the Spirit and changed our designation to Full Gospel Baptist. And I was in transition between leaving the National Baptist Convention and starting the "new thing" God was revealing to me.

As we continued expanding the New Orleans East location we realized it would be better to have a 3,000-seat sanctuary and conduct two services, than to build a 7,000-seat sanctuary and hold one service. That way, we could always go back to one service if needed. It definitely takes the mind of the Lord and strategic, practical discipline to keep changing forward as God expands your territory.

Changing a Generation

God directed me to bring churches and pastors together using the same model that Jesus used when He chose the twelve to start His earthly ministry. God also identified those who would co-labor with me to start His movement. This resulted in the formation of the Full Gospel Baptist Church Fellowship. The time was upon us to change a generation.

I must confess, this was a hard time for me and pushed me far outside my comfort zone. I knew that one of the first people God had told me to approach was Pastor J. D. Wiley from Michigan. He had to leave all he knew and step out on faith; he did.

If Pastor Wiley could find a building, we would renovate it and supply the people to help him get started. Together, we prayerfully announced it to the congregation. We found and renovated a building in the West Bank area of New Orleans, and using our "extra miler" model, a new church was born.

As each new church grew, some "extra milers" came home and others remained to grow in leadership in the new location that might not have been available to them at the "mother church."

Things were happening at Greater St. Stephen! I had the "best of the best," because ministry is more caught than taught. I had a great Elders' Council, which became my right hand in ministry. They had my vision and spirit. Elders, including Robert Taylor, Daryl Brister, Ira Moses, Louis Kelly, and, later, Lester Love, were all in the forefront of our ministry plantings. When God said to plant, I would always send my best.

Ultimately, I sent out many of the original Elders' Council to pastor, and we continued adding more churches. As it became necessary, we would train the next group of leaders and send them out. I constantly sacrificed the best to build God's kingdom.

Then in 2003 we decided the churches that would be birthed out of Greater St. Stephen would be called Changing a Generation FGBC. We planted CAG, Arabi, Louisiana, and CAG in Morgan

City, with Bishop Greg Davis. Then CAG plantings followed in Baton Rouge and Bouitte, Louisiana, and CAG West Bank. My spiritual children made me so proud. After six months of "extra miler" participation each of these churches was handling things on its own. Watching them grow to become the best in their areas brought joy to my heart.

Churches in the city were starting to realize that if they were serious about growth, it was best to get someone who had been trained by Greater St. Stephen. What a blessing! I thank God for surrounding me with spiritual sons who had my spirit and passion. Each of them had the kind of drive that I liked. They were creative, and that made me work harder to do more creative things.

Several of them had given up good salaries at Greater St. Stephen to start new ministries, but I knew the only way they would be successful was to "leave the nest." Greater St. Stephen had become the mother eagle; we were producing eaglets that had the capacity to fly on their own. God had shown me great leadership ability in each of them that they once couldn't see in themselves

If you are waiting to be released into ministry, allow me to give you a word of advice. Listen to your pastor. If he or she tells you that you're not ready to leave the nest, be patient. The Bible teaches we should obey the counsel of our spiritual leaders. If you try to jump out on your own before your pastor thinks you're ready, your ministry could fail. Patience is a virtue, especially in the kingdom of God.

Birthing the Full Gospel Baptist Church Fellowship

I knew that I couldn't reach my full potential only through Greater St. Stephen. In time, I resigned from the Ideal Missionary

Baptist Association (which was part of the National Baptist Convention), where I had served as second Vice President. I knew God didn't want me to bring confusion or cause a split inside the convention, and I refused to become disloyal.

It was difficult for me to share with key colleagues why I was leaving, but I explained that I couldn't serve the association any longer because God had sent me to something that was totally different from what was being taught according to traditional Baptist doctrine.

We continued expanding God's new movement, which birthed the Full Gospel Baptist Church Fellowship. Once again, I was reminded of Jesus' leadership model: identifying twelve leaders to form the foundation. God promised that He would surround me with the right people.

The first of "the twelve" was Reverend Odis Floyd from Flint, Michigan. Floyd was like a big brother to me. He had also led an effort several years earlier of pastors who were seeking to "free their churches" from traditional Baptist norms. They were called "Free Spirit" churches. It took a lot of nerve for me to ask him to become my Second Presiding Bishop. He had raised up more pastors than I had. I shared everything with him that God had put in my spirit. This included my burden to take Baptists to the next level and give them the "right to choose" to operate in the gifts of the Spirit in the Baptist church. I also told him that God had told me to change our titles to "Bishop" to be more biblically sound.

Then for a few moments I allowed my flesh to reign, because I knew God had told me to lead this movement, but I told Reverend Floyd that I would be his backup man; he had more experience in this area. I offered to help him find the twelve men to organize it, and I would assume the title of Second Presiding Bishop. At that time, he always called me "Bud." He said emphatically, "No way, Bud. This is a 'God thing' that He gave you. *I* will work with *you!*" I firmly believe he saved me from getting in trouble with God.

I was excited. This was a new beginning. I immediately began to fast and pray about how God wanted us to do this thing.

God started bringing pastors together, some who knew me and others who didn't. Many of them were willing to take both personal and denominational risks, to face hardship and ridicule, to try something that had never been done before.

There were so many gifts among the twelve. Pastor Andy Lewter and Pastor Gregory Davis came in to help with the organizing, setting up regions and districts in the United States. Pastor Lewter and Pastor Kenneth Ulmer (from California) developed our Statement of Purpose, which became the *Full Gospel Distinctives.* Later, my spiritual son, Pastor Tommie Triplett joined the group and added his unique gifts. Pastor Larry Trotter from Chicago; Pastor Jesse Gavin from Pennsylvania; and Pastor A. R. Williams (the brother of Dr. Jasper Williams) from Memphis, Tennessee, also joined.

The list continued to grow through associations God had put in place earlier in my ministry, including Pastor Kenneth Robinson from Little Rock, Arkansas; Pastor Larry Leonard from Houston, Texas; and Pastor K. D. Johnson from Memphis.

God was making the connections that would allow His movement to grow and take on a national flavor. At the same time, I was preaching regularly on Black Entertainment Television (BET), which airs across the nation, but it struck a nerve with many of the viewers because I was a Baptist preacher talking about the fullness of the Holy Ghost.

Undaunted, I announced that I would come to any city to share with any pastor about the movement. In fact, if a pastor wanted to organize other pastors for a breakfast or luncheon meeting at my expense, they could be my guests. The phone began ringing off the hook. There were some disappointments in several of those cities, but God was advancing the vision.

Renowned author, John Maxwell, put it best when he said there are some who are "natural born leaders."[1] Among the twelve who were chosen to lead the Full Gospel Baptist Church Fellowship, I believe I had the "best of the natural born leaders." They caught the vision and ran with it. It was a difficult challenge to approach twelve men who *already* had a vision and tell them I needed them to participate in my vision. I believe in the kingdom of God, a key to success in ministry is participating in someone else's dream.

Interestingly, when word got out that I was involved in organizing this movement, there were local repercussions. I was black-balled in New Orleans. After having developed great relationships with many pastors and churches, some of the twelve were being categorically disenfranchised because of their association with me. I asked God: "Why me?" I knew He had to have a greater plan.

A few weeks later, a prophet I didn't know came to my office and said: "God told me to tell you that He has called you to be an apostle. You will open up new paths and become a trailblazer. Ministries will be formed out of you." I thought he was referring to the Full Gospel movement, and if that was the case, he was a little late. He was right, because God used him to confirm to me that I was beginning to walk in an apostolic anointing.

Consecrating the Movement

As I've already mentioned, God told me change my title from "Elder" to "Bishop." To this end, my consecration service at Greater St. Stephen took place on March 19, 1993. First Timothy 3:1 says, "If a man desires the position of a bishop, he desires a good work." I had a deep appreciation for this, because I had to work, and work hard.

Bishops from different reformations came to confirm what God was doing. Bishop C. L. Morton, my eldest brother, from the Church of God in Christ, conducted the service. Bishop Charles E. Blake, who is now the Presiding Bishop of the Church of God in Christ, preached the message. It was a powerful prophetic word! I'll never forget it. He called it, "A New Structure on an Old Foundation."

We had been laboring in "God's Movement" by creating a new structure on the old foundation. We still believed in the death, burial, and resurrection of our Lord and Savior, Jesus Christ. The "new structure" was the power of the Holy Ghost, operating through the gifts of the Spirit, and the first African-American Baptist Bishop with a large following. This was truly a "new thing"! He took his text from Isaiah 43:19: "Behold, I will do a new thing, now it shall spring forth; shall you not know it? I will even make a road in the wilderness and rivers in the desert."

It was time for me as Presiding Bishop to consecrate "the twelve." I appointed four officers and made the other members of the Council Regional or Auxiliary Bishops to develop states and districts. After that event, new people began contacting us every day, interested in joining the fellowship. We rose to the challenge to open a pathway in the wilderness.

When you are blazing a new path you have to expect and endure hardships along the way. There will be difficulties, criticisms, and at times you will feel alone. The "new thing" that was taking place in the FGBCF was considered "impossible" according to the people, but nothing is impossible with God.

We scheduled our first conference for July 1994, Greater St. Stephen supported me as I traveled the length and breadth of the country. This was a God thing!

Whenever God is moving in a mighty way, move with the cloud. When God delivered the children of Israel out of Egypt, they only knew where to go by following His presence in "a pillar of cloud" by day and a "pillar of fire" by night (see Exodus 13:21). When the cloud stood still, they pitched their tents, rested and ate. When the word came that the cloud was moving, they had to pack everything quickly and move with the cloud. If they didn't, they would have been lost in the wilderness.

This is how God's movement in me, in Greater St. Stephen, and in the FGBCF has endured the test of time. He keeps doing something new and fresh as we remain sensitive to His voice. He'll do the same for you. No matter how difficult it may seem at first, you can change forward and press through God's "so that" process.

Facing a Family Tragedy

The devil was mad because a major move of God was breaking forth in the earth realm. As we approached our first FGBCF Conference, my older sister Nancy died of cancer at forty-six years of age. Nancy had a powerful anointing on her life and was a gifted minister who served as my administrator at Greater St. Stephen. She knew what I needed and flowed in a spirit of excellence.

I was never reluctant to use family members in the ministry, if they had the skills and talent. Growing up in a "first family" had its challenges, including facing jealousy from church members. At times, they made us step back so that others wouldn't get angry, even though we could have performed a task better. I decided early in my ministry I was not going to allow that to happen.

Nancy's death was very difficult for me. I was frequently at her bedside in our home, praying her back from death, even when she was saying, "Let me go." Then one day I left to preach in another city and she passed. It was as if she had said, "My brother is gone; let me get out of here before he gets back." Debra and I raised Nancy's three sons, two of whom became preachers and are working with me in the ministry and one is pursuing a singing career.

My sister Gwen took over Nancy's duties with the same amount of excellence. Later, when my daughter Jasmine graduated from Spellman College in Atlanta, she became the assistant administrator. Even when we have to deal with issues, we've always maintained that we have each other's backs.

No doubt, the devil was trying to drain me when Nancy left this earth, but I was determined not to let that happen. The joy of the Lord was my strength and the congregation was my support. I thank God for it, because the first Full Gospel Baptist Church Fellowship Conference was at hand. I set my eyes on the Lord and kept moving forward.

CHAPTER SEVENTEEN

LOSING TO GAIN

We had worked hard for an entire year, sharing the vision of Full Gospel with the world. We had talked about it on our BET telecasts, and our Full Gospel family had been spreading the news, inviting others to see what God was doing in the Baptist church. Initially, we planned to hold the convention at Greater St. Stephen, which would seat three thousand. Then we moved to the UNO Lakefront Arena in New Orleans, which would seat ten thousand. Finally, we had to change our plans to meet at the Louisiana Superdome. When we finally met, there were over twenty-five thousand people in the arena, praising God. The Holy Spirit was present in that place.

Those first years, the conference ran five days and nights without stopping. The good people of Greater St. Stephens carried the load of volunteering in the first years and over time others stepped up to help. From the third year on, we changed to a three day format.

And always, we sought the Lord's guidance on what to do and how to do it. You can't step out on your own strength, but only rely upon Him.

Shifts in the Leadership

After the first couple of years, we began to experience rifts with some of our leaders. God had called us to raise a standard and change a generation. Now the founding fathers were re-addressing and resolving some theological differences in our Bishop's Council meetings. The most serious was the purpose of the Holy Ghost and speaking in tongues.

For me, there was no need to debate whether speaking in tongues was a "qualifier" of receiving the Holy Ghost baptism. We had already agreed that it was an "indicator." There had to be some "signs" or manifestations that a person had received this baptism (Mark 16:17-18); however, the key was receiving "power" according to Acts 1:8. When we're filled with God's power, we can get beyond natural thinking. It's like a pot of water on a stove. When it gets hot enough, it bubbles over. You can see and hear it happening. When we get "filled" beyond our natural intellect, the Holy Ghost begins to speak and move through us—and we get supernatural results.

This disagreement burdened me because there was no way the dissenting council members could support the vision, when they didn't agree with its foundational principles. So, though we had become "full gospel," several bishops still held to their traditional beliefs. If this persisted, we could no longer change forward; we would start changing backward, and that wasn't my assignment.

For certain, God had been good to us. God's new movement through the Full Gospel Baptist Church Fellowship was making an immediate, widespread impact. It was hard for me to lose some of my closest associates—men I had thought would be in the movement for life. Two of the Bishop's Council members, who believed as I believed, ended up leaving the fellowship. Confusion had come into the camp, and though I knew what I believed, I didn't want any trouble. I urged my colleagues to lighten up, because I didn't want to lose anyone else. But this was a compromising position. In order for God's movement to function the way He intended, the key leaders had to fully support the cause.

Proving God's "So That" Process

God wasn't surprised by any of these developments. I just had to focus on Him and let my spirit rule over my mind. God helped me to realize that He had put certain people in place to validate the movement and help get it started.

Now, it appeared that everything was falling apart. God reminded me, everything that's big isn't necessarily good. "Big" doesn't always mean healthy. Although some of the original members left, most of the people they had drawn into the fellowship stayed.

Then God made it clear, if the fellowship was going to expand its territory and bring about great change, we would have to lose in order to gain.

Though I didn't want the original members to leave, He gave me peace that some things were just meant to be. If I was going to be God's change agent, I had to expect changes would come.

God is proving our faith as we learn to believe and obey Him in the midst of confusing paradoxes and difficult circumstances. Each time we keep our eyes on Him, instead of focusing on our problems, we gain insight and change forward. God's "so that" process is absolutely necessary in our lives.

I came to grips with the fact that God knew everything that was coming down the pike before it happened. I knew "all things work together for good to them that love God, to them who are the called according to His purpose" (Romans 8:28 KJV). The problems we were facing in the council didn't mean God had lost control. Rather, they were giving us a glorious opportunity to prove His "so that" principle.

More Leadership Changes

It was clear that we needed to create a second tier of leadership. John Maxwell referred to this tier as "trained leaders."[1] This tier of leadership would be vitally important to the movement changing forward. We had to bear in mind as we expanded our ranks that there would be many new ideas, which is good, but there could be only *one* vision.

The fellowship was new and fresh, and people wanted to get involved. I knew it was going to be a struggle to mesh. I met a young man after the first conference, who was so excited about joining the fellowship. He invited me to come and preach to his congregation and by the time I got home, I found out that he had been summarily dismissed from that church. It about broke my heart that this happened but he listened to the Lord and planted a church in Roanoke, Virginia. It became one of the greatest churches in the fellowship. In time, he became a state overseer and eventually became the Regional Bishop of the Southern Atlantic Region.

We really had to do spiritual warfare. Becoming a bishop isn't about a title; it's about doing the work. Some wanted the title without doing the work. They came into the fellowship expecting to be immediately consecrated to the office. If they weren't, they were gone just as quickly as they came. I was determined that the standard of ecclesiastical behavior we upheld in the FGBCF would be at the highest level. A "trained leader" had to be saved, sanctified, and filled with the Holy Ghost. In addition, he or she had to possess good character and be willing to do a "good work."

God blessed us with many trained leaders but who were untrained in the Full Gospel distinctive. They needed to be retrained. They would learn to know me in order to share the spirit and burden God had given me for the fellowship. In other words, they would have the same love for God, as well as the same degree of love and concern for the people.

Finally, John Maxwell also stated there are "limited leaders."[2] Some of these people don't know how to lead, but have the passion to learn. Others have a passion to learn, but don't have the ability to get people to follow them. Though they are limited in their gift, they're faithful. Many times, God uses these people in powerful ways.

Many times, being "faithful" is better than being "talented," because it's often difficult to depend on those who possess talent only. Both "natural born" and "trained" leaders can become lifted up in pride, and as a result, become less dependable. On the other hand, the "limited" leader will tell you up front when he or she doesn't know something, but is willing to learn. The bottom line is that true leaders aren't discovered. True leaders—natural born, trained or limited—are developed.

Keeping Focused on the Vision

One of my favorite books is *Who's Holding Your Ladder?* by Dr. Samuel Chand. In his introduction, he explains that he came up with the title of his book while watching a man standing on a ladder, painting. He couldn't take his eyes off of him, as he moved the brush and roller across the surface of the wall. Then he noticed the painter was only covering a limited area. He had stretched as far as he could to the right and left, and even above his head. But he didn't use the whole ladder.

Why didn't this painter reach higher? Because there was no one to hold the ladder. By himself, the painter couldn't go any higher. He had done all that he could do by himself, but to stretch beyond his comfort zone, he needed help.[3]

I learned a valuable lesson from that story. As I considered the growth of the Full Gospel Baptist Church Fellowship, I knew that the effectiveness of my leadership as Presiding Bishop depended on the people who were holding the ladder. Even though I was the visionary, the heights God would allow us to reach would be influenced and controlled by who was holding the ladder.

The people whom God was adding to the fellowship as bishops, overseers and pastors (as well as in the other tiers of leadership) were just as important to the success and effectiveness of the FGBCF as I was.

We were planting churches from Greater St. Stephen. Since then, as the "mother eagle," we had spread our wings even wider to establish the FGBCF. God had taken us deeper in His vision and higher on His ladder. So, I had made it my practice as we were expanding to regularly speak into the lives of our leadership. I firmly believe this is one of the reasons our church and fellowship are so strong.

Once a month, I speak to the members of our Full Gospel family through regional conference calls. Not only does it develop strong leaders, it maintains our focus on God's vision for the FGBCF. I also mentor a group of about forty spiritual sons and daughters who pastor on a monthly basis. I take my leadership roles very seriously.

I understand that I am the visionary and the ladder is the vision. As I seek and obey God, the vision continues to expand; it keeps reaching higher and wider. I could have received the best training in the world, but like that painter, my own blend of expertise and passion aren't enough to complete the whole picture. Those who work with me will determine the heights to which God's movement can ultimately go.

CHAPTER EIGHTEEN

THE COLLATERAL DAMAGE OF SPIRITUAL WARFARE

In 1998, I had my greatest test in trying to move forward. Because of the rapid growth and broad acceptance of the Full Gospel Fellowship, the conference became one of the largest held in America. I wanted the fellowship to have an impact both spiritually and economically and believed that much could have been accomplished by working together.

The "idea" was for the Fellowship to have its own bank (E Line Banking), to which we could invest and give our support. A group called, *Compunomics*, claimed to have a great idea that I thought would help the Fellowship be on the cutting edge of business and investments. To get it off the ground, some of us were asked to invest $1,000, $5,000, or $10,000. All through my life, I thought I was too smart for someone to take advantage of me. However, these people were criminals and *Compunomics* was a scam. It caused me to have a nervous breakdown. I was seriously tested and I talked freely about it in one of my books, *Why Kingdoms Fall*.

As a minister of the gospel, my assignment in the Kingdom of God is to preach the good news of Jesus Christ and to destroy the works of the devil. I had been doing that for years, but when the critical hour came, I found myself unready for the intense battle of spiritual warfare that was about to occur. I was out of order! Yes, I said, I was out of order. I knew the "Divine Order" of God was the Spirit over the mind. I knew that if it were mind over the Spirit in any situation, there would be disorder. Whenever there is disorder, there is going to be a breakdown and a breakdown with God necessitates a breakthrough. This was serious warfare on the battlefield of my mind.

Spiritual warfare began in the Garden of Eden. There were two trees in the garden: the Tree of Life, which represented the Spirit and the Tree of the Knowledge of Good and Evil, which represented the mind. There was a command from God for Adam and Eve to leave the Tree of the Knowledge of Good and Evil alone. In other words, it was out of order to lean to your mind rather than to the Spirit. To do so made a breakdown inevitable.

The e-bank organizers took our money and ran. It hurt me not just because I and the others in our organization lost money. The newspaper headlines showed no mercy and depicted me as an inept leader. Greater St. Stephen, after twenty years, knew me and knew that I was a man of integrity. I had been very careful previously in making good investments—but, I had only been Presiding Bishop of Full Gospel Baptist Church Fellowship for a few years. Would they ever trust me again to help them change forward?

Of course, after the breakdown, I found out that they did and that they were able to see that it was not my fault. We did everything we could do to pay back every investor. I paid much of it out of my own pocket. I tried diligently to pay it back before I had the breakdown, but the devil was still messing with my mind.

The greatest thing a leader can have is his influence, and it is a sacred trust. It doesn't matter about how popular or gifted you are, if you lose your influence, you lose your ability to lead. The worst thing that can happen in your life is for God to "fire" you and you not know that you're fired.

The scam had occurred early in our efforts to get investors, and there were many who had not had time to join in the effort. I had paid back most of those who had lost money with me but, I was overwhelmed and burdened with the idea that my good name was tied to this failed investment and the devil used the weapon of "pride" on me.

The Securities and Exchange Commission was involved. The Commission let me know that it was not my fault and that they had been in pursuit of the criminals for a long while. Even after the government cleared me, I continued to try to find every piece of paper and every transaction to prove what they had already determined, namely my innocence. Although God continued to remind me that He was in charge of protecting my name, I was not listening. I couldn't sleep or eat. I was convinced that Full Gospel would no longer follow my leadership. The pressure became too great and my mind snapped!

Two Christian psychologists, Dr. Frank Minirth and Dr. Paul Meier, said, in their jointly written book, *Happiness Is a Choice*,[1] that there are three major reasons for clinical depression, which was the ultimate medical diagnosis for my breakdown. They are: lack of self-worth, lack of intimacy with others, and lack of intimacy with God.

The devil had been attacking me with questions that had brought down my level of self-worth. I felt worthless! That's what the devil will try to do to you. You make a mistake and he will make you believe it's the end of the world!

I also had to come to terms regarding my intimacy with *others*. I had to go deep in my heart because losing my father at such a young age had made me a loner. I have always had a hard time trusting people. My wife would ask me to tell her what was on my mind. Perhaps I would have been dealing with church problems, budgets, and so on, and she would make me open up, saying, "We are in this together." I had friends who would trust me to share their thoughts, struggles, and dreams. I was a good listener, but couldn't reciprocate. In fact, I was a shy person who tried to find ways of covering up my shyness.

However, the part of Minirth and Meier's book that was most difficult for me to digest dealt with lack of intimacy with God. I really had to look at myself because it had become obvious that even though I had been close to God, this situation had caused me to turn away from Him. I had such a driving force within me to see this bank succeed for my people, it became as if I were telling God, "I got this. I don't need you to direct me on this. I know this is great!" I messed up "big time"!

I suffered all the physical symptoms of depression; sleeping all day, overeating, anxieties, and unreliability became the routine. The most serious of the symptoms of depression, delusional thinking, occurs in severe cases. The delusional thinker is clearly out of touch with reality. They hear and see things that just aren't there and become extremely suspicious and paranoid, believing everyone is out to get them.

According to my doctors, I reached the level of delusional thinking, seeing things that were not actually there.

It was clear to me that I was fighting a battle in the spiritual realm, and I was out of order because I was not listening to the Spirit.

My wife fought the enemy with and for me throughout the whole ordeal. When she started talking to me about going to the doctor, I screamed at her, "No!" The devil made me believe that "good" doctors were "bad." I refused to listen to Debra, to go to the doctor, to do anything but look to my own strength. I knew God uses doctors for His purpose, but I had lost my ability to see that.

The Lord led me into the wilderness for forty days. It was very much similar to the experiences of Jesus, recorded in Matthew 4:1 (TLB): "Then Jesus was led into the wilderness by the Holy Spirit to be tempted there by Satan. Jesus went into the wilderness willingly out of obedience."

I did finally seek help from a doctor and I'm so grateful that there are those in the medical field, who when they know that it's beyond their ability, they will call for some "spiritual people" to help them. These good doctors know that you can have something from which you cannot be delivered in the natural, but need both their help and spiritual help. I had allowed my own thinking to get out of sync with God's order.

Throughout all of my time in ministry, I have believed in following God's order. I would rebuke the devil if he tried to tempt me. However, this time, I thought God was taking too long to handle my situation. I tried to take matters into my own hands by rebuking and calling out the demons that were tormenting me.

God was teaching me how to win against the devil by discerning and being sensitive to His voice only. If I had listened to Him and obeyed Him, I would have been victorious over the devil every time.

I was becoming exhausted because the enemy would not allow me to sleep or rest. I finally let Debra take me to the hospital.

I now know, that my breakdown was a major "so that" moment in my life. I believe that God allowed me to go through it so that in turn, I would be able to communicate this invaluable lesson to the church so that we all might experience victory in this area. It is imperative that we have ears to hear what the Spirit of the Lord is saying and to obey Him.

I was told that many who go through this kind of experience become permanently psychotic. I believe it was only because I was born again and spiritually knowledgeable that the experience of my breakdown was different. Under the guidance of the Holy Spirit, I was able to clearly see many of the things that I went through. God had forewarned me that if I allowed my mind to get ahead of my spirit, I would lose touch with reality. I made errors in judgment, but I committed my mind to Him.

Through every one of those experiences, God kept me in His grace. This allowed me to make mistakes without suffering irreparable damage to my psyche. Changing forward, I was able to see more clearly in the spirit realm and He showed me so many things that others could not see. He showed it to me because he had called me to fill that need in the earth realm.

The gift that God had given me was that of discernment. It's difficult for anyone to fool you when you have that gift. Regardless of how much they smile, cry, give, or talk. From that experience, I received the gift of humility. I was determined never again to try and get ahead of Him. It's for this reason, I tell people that the Spirit of the Lord led me in the wilderness—that unknown realm—to be tempted by the devil, but from that wilderness experience, I would learn valuable lessons that will help other people change forward. It was my experience with God and my yielding to the power of God that has brought me safe thus far.

The message from Drs. Minirth and Meier is clear in its emphasis: *"Every human will suffer temporary grief reactions* from time to time, but if a person puts into practice the knowledge he gains . . . , *there is no reason why he should ever get clinically depressed,* unless he has a genetic bipolar disorder, which occurs in only 1 percent of the population. For the other 99 percent, happiness, in the long run, will be his choice."[2]

Happiness is a choice. For many years, I was in the 99 percent who had no problem. Happiness was my choice. Yet, in the hospital, I was diagnosed as being in that one percent who had bipolar disorder, for which well-respected physicians declared there was no cure. My doctor explained to me the seriousness of the disorder and the number of people who had been affected by its effects. "Bi" means two and the condition is like having two poles in your head—one pole is an "anxiety pole" and the other is a "depression pole." He added that with the aid of doctors and the right medication, the condition could be controlled.

I was prescribed medicine to calm me down, and manage the extreme highs and lows of the disorder and prevent the potential of suicide. That was never a thought that came up in my mind throughout the entire ordeal, but they were operating in the natural. In all fairness, they also said that my strong gifted side could kick in and cause me to go mad! Only this medicine would give me balance.

I was told that I would have to continue taking that medicine the rest of my life. The other and only option for me was to be balanced by Jesus. I decided to let Jesus balance me. The word is affirmed in Isaiah 26:3: "Thou will keep him in perfect peace, whose mind is stayed on thee, because he trusteth in thee" (KJV).

This is the promise to everyone who meets the conditions of keeping their mind stayed on Jesus and who will trust in Him at all times in all things and in all places: "Peace Guaranteed." We have to understand that peace is not freedom from trouble. How, then, can peace be identified? It must be identified with the presence of God. We must be drawn into a close union with God and often that kind of spiritual positioning brings trouble.

Our ultimate security is the faithfulness of God—His unchangeable love, power, and understanding. The peace in which the believer is kept perfect, complete, satisfied, and matured is capable of sustaining any test. When you are really in the presence of God, neither the enemy nor your circumstances will matter.

It was clear to me, if not to anyone else, that the battle for me was not medical. I was fighting a battle I knew was spiritual. It does not matter how educated or uneducated you are, your educated mind can still kill the word of God, until it sounds foolish to you. If, on the other hand, you receive with the spirit over the mind, you will be victorious.

I needed to listen to the Spirit. Self had to die. It had to be Him and not "me." In that spiritual realm, I died. The Spirit of the Lord took me through the process and broke me down so that I could rebuild to change a generation. In order to prepare myself for spiritual warfare and to be the "Positive Change Agent" God had called me to be, I had to go through a spiritual fight.

The doctors suggested to me that my illness could not be healed because it had passed down through my genes. I had a problem with that information coming from the doctors because first, there is no disorder in God. There is no breakdown in Him.

The doctors were saying that there was "no cure" and that I had to accept that and live with it. I said, "No, I don't receive that!" The Bible says that if an angel from heaven comes preaching something contrary to God's word, we shouldn't accept it. Thus, even if a noted psychiatrist comes preaching something, with all of his degrees that is contrary to the word of God, I would not accept it.

It is a mistake to believe that if our world were free of trouble, our hearts would be free. The psalmist cried, "Oh that I had wings like a dove, then would I fly away." The fact of the matter is that it would have been all in vain for me to do that. Wherever we go, we must carry ourselves. It is not what's out there that can make or break you; it's what's in the heart.

When I came out of my breakdown, I was on a whole new level. There was no more compromising in order to keep folks who didn't believe what God had told me to do happy. My assignment was to declare that this movement was to usher in the power of the Holy Ghost into the Baptist Church and to let Baptists know that they could receive these spiritual gifts.

I stood before God and repented. I stood before Full Gospel and declared that the Fellowship must stand regardless of who didn't like it. I had my instructions from God and He didn't have to tell me twice. All I could see was changing forward.

Although we are new creatures in Christ Jesus, we still have to fight temptation. The old sinful nature fights against our inner man, and if we fail to resist, it causes us to become weaker and weaker.

The devil comes with accusations that appeal to our pride. He will detect subtle forms of pride in us by suggesting that "no one appreciates what you do" or that people in the church are "mistreating you." He will let you become puffed up only to take you down and bring false accusations against you. He will infer that God doesn't appreciate you and if He did, He wouldn't allow you to go through the things that you go through. It's for this reason we must be able to come against the enemy's lies.

CHAPTER NINETEEN

GOD'S ORDER

When you obey the Spirit, you are in order. The Holy Spirit does not want you to "die before your time" or before you have lived the full and successful life that God has planned for you. We blame things on God for some of the foolish things we do. That is why I have chosen to set the record straight in this book.

In every area of your life, you must be careful to not allow your mind to tell you something contrary to the Holy Spirit or God's word. Don't listen to the lies, enticements, and deceptions of the enemy. Listen to the Spirit and take God at His word. That's the key to changing forward. The devil's ultimate goal in the life of a Christian is to make sure our thinking prevails over the voice of God. When he achieves that, he renders us ineffective and powerless in the work of the Kingdom.

In the realm of spiritual warfare, we can become wounded soldiers, barely hanging on to life. We must defeat the devil's efforts to take us out of the battle. To accomplish that, we must learn his subtle tactics and weapons. The devil always comes against Christians with at least three weapons: temptation, accusations, and deception. He uses them in subtle ways that can sometimes fool even the most mature Christian.

Through temptation, the devil appeals to the lust of the flesh. He knows what we like; he knows what feels good to us and it's not just sex. He knows that we're tempted to gain power, influence, money, position, attention and so forth by any means available. Satan knows from experience to hit us in our soft or weak spots. If we love money, for example, he will tempt you to steal and cheat and have you hope to escape discovery. If we have a tendency to lie, he will always put us in a position where it is profitable and easy to do.

Perhaps one of the most subtle of Satan's temptations is that of casting doubt on the word of God. Satan knows the word and will come after you in the same way that he came after Eve and Jesus, attempting to trick you into doubting or changing the word. In Genesis 3, Satan tempted Eve by casting doubt upon what God had spoken to her and Adam. "Did God really say . . . ? Then Satan proceeded to reconfigure both the words and the intent of God, which might be paraphrased: "Eve, that's not true. You will not surely die. God does not want you to eat from the tree of Knowledge of Good and Evil because He knows that the moment that you do, your eyes will become open to good and evil and you will be as smart as God." That happens today when people consider themselves, in their educated minds, to be smarter than God and His word.

The devil is still using the same tricks and we must be mindful of them. Eve had received God's word "second-hand" from Adam and she added a little of her own opinion when she conveyed to Satan the instructions that had been given. Satan knew he had her on "shaky ground." Not only must we thoroughly study the Bible for ourselves in order to know exactly what God said, but we must guard against Satan's constant attempts to cast doubt on the word, causing you to go backward.

Matthew 5:9-11 reads: "Blessed are the peacemakers: for they shall be called the children of God. Blessed are they which are persecuted for righteousness' sake: for theirs is the kingdom of heaven. Blessed are ye when men shall revile you, and persecute you, and shall say all manner of evil against you falsely, for my sake" (KJV).

In Scripture, these verses make up what is called the "Beatitudes." The "Beatitudes" in Ebonics is "How your attitude be?" Each virtue in the Beatitudes has its own appropriate blessing. Those who hunger and thirst after righteousness are filled. Those who mourn are comforted, and the pure in heart shall see God. The peacemakers are called the sons of God—a special relationship and a place of position.

It is the "peacemaker" who is declared to be a "child of God." The Bible does not say that it is the "peaceable." Peaceable people will see someone stealing furniture from the house next door but elect to remain silent about it, not wanting to get involved because they are "peaceable." Peacemakers do not accept things as they are, nor "leave well enough alone."

There are preachers who will elect not to preach against "sin," because it will work against the peace. They will subscribe to what I call the "Rodney King Doctrine": "Why can't we all get along?" It's a false peace. Keeping peace merely to make people happy won't work. Your relationship with God can become dysfunctional. It's false. People will seek peace instead of truth, but truth brings peace. Know the truth and the truth will make you free.

Peacemakers are resolute and uncompromising fighters against every disturbing and disruptive force. That means that they are enemies of all evil that is disturbing and disruptive (false peace).

Jesus said, "My peace I leave with you, but not as the world gives it." You may be left with a "Gethsemane moment," where you have to wrestle in your personal garden of prayer. "Lord, if it be Your will, let this cup pass, because I really don't want to deal with this conflict. Nevertheless, not my will, but Your will be done." Sometimes, the peace that Jesus leaves with you leads you to "your personal Calvary," where they will crucify you, but the good news is that if it's truth and for the sake of the gospel, you will rise again. No weapon that is formed against you shall prosper.

Note that the peacemakers are not the meek of the second beatitude found in Matthew 5. The meek are those who do not return evil for evil. Peacemakers are those who replace good for evil, even though they may be persecuted. Peacemakers establish peace in the time of war. When Jesus said that He had come to bring "war" not peace, He meant war against evil, against Satan, and the world. War against evil is an offense against Satan, the murderer. It is war against the world where strife reigns eternally. In a word, Jesus meant to wage "war against war." To be a peacemaker, we must fight in peace as well as for peace. That's real peace!

You must beware of the devil's tricks because he is a master at deception. Once accusation and pride take root in a Christian's life, a subtle form of deception follows. Romans 12:3 says: "For I say, through the grace given unto me, to every man that is among you, not to think of himself more highly than he ought to think, but to think soberly, according as God hath dealt to every man the measure of faith" (KJV).

We have received from God the grace—the unmerited favor of God—that was bestowed upon us. It was not because we were so good or wonderful. It was just His grace. Whatever gift we have and no matter how great it is, God merely loaned it to us. It's not ours.

God uses humble people but the devil uses proud people. When we are deceived with pride, Satan gets the glory rather than God.

One of the problems that we face in the church is that the higher we go, the less accountable we become because we think we are all that! I teach that every pastor needs a "pastor" or someone to whom he can be accountable. You can tend to become so big that you don't feel obligated to answer to anyone because you grew your ministry or you made it what it has become. You need to know that any growth that occurred during your tenure was by the grace of God.

In the Full Gospel Baptist Church Fellowship, even as International Presiding Bishop, I hold myself accountable to the Bishop's Council. At Changing a Generation, Atlanta, I hold myself accountable to my brother, Bishop James Morton, as my pastor, because, first, he's not afraid to tell me the truth. It is essential for us to bring humility back into the pulpit.

After my breakdown, I sat myself down for thirty days. I had not stolen anything. I was totally innocent of the e-bank matter and had been cleared of any wrongdoing by the Securities and Exchange Commission, but I have always taught myself the "order of God"— keeping the Spirit over the mind. Yet, I allowed the devil to give me a breakdown. I should have practiced what I preached. I did finally repent and promised my church that, as long as I lived, I would not have another breakdown. Changing forward, God promised to keep me in perfect peace, if I kept my mind staid on Him. That was "Guaranteed Peace!"

There was no denying that there were loyal church members, who in 1998, let me know that it was unnecessary for me to sit down, because they understood that it was not my fault, but the body of Christ needs to see humility in its leaders. It also was necessary to let the members know that I was going to be as hard on me as I would have been on them, when they were wrong. You can't bring people forward with tied hands.

We must believe God's word. When we sin, there should be a compelling desire to repent. When there is sin, we must be eager to repent. Matthew 3:8 reads, "Bring forth therefore, fruits meet for repentance." In other words, you need to show that you are really sorry for what you have done. Rather than acting as though nothing has happened, show some signs.

Luke 17:3-4 reads: "Take heed to yourselves: if thy brother trespass against thee, rebuke him; and if he repent, forgive him. And if he trespass against thee seven times in a day, and seven times in a day, turn again to thee saying, 'I repent,' thou shalt forgive him" (KJV).

Because we can't serve as God and judge, we must forgive. We must also repent. If we follow the order of God, He is "God of a second chance." You cannot count the number of chances He has given you. Everything hinges on repentance.

We have to become more accountable. It seems that there is some level of accountability for everyone, except, those of us in the pulpit. I am a living witness that people will lie about you and that is why the Bible calls for the presence of two or three witnesses that every word be established. I want the Lord to do whatever it takes to bring me into order.

There is a sermon that I preach titled, "Successful Sin." There is no denying that I love success. I believe most people love success, but it all depends upon the kind of success. Success is defined as "meeting in accordance with a desire." Desire differs among human beings. For some, it's pleasure for wealth, and for others, it is to please God. Now, that's true success!

In one of the more desperate and frustrating periods of Job's trials, he said, "The wicked gather the vintage" (Job 24:6). It sometimes seems as though the most wicked and evil people get the best, the good, and the quality, while the child of God gets the leftovers. There are times when sin feels good! The devil will tempt you with what you like and what you need. With Jesus, it was food, when He was hungry. "Turn these stones into bread," the devil challenged Him. Jesus was accustomed to power, but he was urged "Jump down from the pinnacle of the temple; the angels will save you." The devil knows what you like.

By the same token, the devil will mess with you while you are dreaming, if he can't deal with you while you are awake. You can be sleeping beside your wife, whom you love, with no desire for anyone else. Yet, you wake up saying, "Halle!" Listen, you had better add a "lujah" to that word quickly—make it "hallelujah" or you will be in a world of trouble.

"Successful sin" blocks our highest beliefs. Sin of any kind has a tendency to spoil the inward vision. It makes it difficult to see the things unseen. While all sin destroys, damages, and darkens the soul, "successful sin" does it in a special way.

Sin that is allowed to prosper confuses the moral senses. When sin fails to bring immediate loss and pain, we get comfortable. When it enjoys immunity and gets away, we are inclined to regard the existence and sovereignty of God as mere "superstition." It is not unusual to hear the refrain: "You see, I told you there was nothing to that and nothing would happen to me."

The prophet, Isaiah, in chapter 5:20-21 says: "Woe unto them that call evil good and good evil, that put darkness for light, and light for darkness, that put bitter for sweet and sweet for bitter. Woe unto them that are wise in their own eyes and prudent in their own sight" (KJV).

We are living in a time where we think we can break all of the rules that God has laid down for us with impunity. He is God and He does not change. God instituted marriage and it is honorable in His sight. If it were not honorable in His sight, we wouldn't do it. The honor is a man for a woman and a woman for a man. That's plain in His word. Because of our pseudo-wisdom and prudence in our own sight, we have chosen to change the intent, purpose, and order for marriage to fit our personal versions of acceptability. We actually think that we are able to get away with this mutation of God's order. If God was displeased with same-sex marriages in Sodom and Gomorrah and allowed it to be destroyed, what makes you think He has changed His mind?

When have we seen so many floods, hurricanes, fires, birds falling from the skies, with no viable explanations for these occurrences? We live in the most powerful nation, but look what's happening to it! God is trying to tell us something. It is almost a travesty when something like 9/11 takes place and everybody joins in the singing of "God Bless America." God has blessed America already; it's time for America to bless God!

Sin, when "successful," is dangerous because it seduces you into greater sin. When you rob the corner grocery store and get away with it, there is a sense of confidence that comes over you to rob something bigger, like a bank. When you are successful with "smoking weed," it can spawn confidence to handle "crack." One successful lie leads to bigger lies.

There is an old saying which goes: "One man can steal a horse and get away with it, while another is arrested for looking over the fence." You ought to thank God for getting caught looking over the fence. "I was about to do it, but I got caught!" It's better if you get caught by someone you respect while doing something wrong, than to "successfully" do it and contract an incurable disease.

Please understand that regardless of how it appears, "no sin is ever successful." It is always superficial and temporary in its appearance. The devil will set you up. Job 24:24-25 sets the framework for this understanding when it says: "They are exalted for a little while, but are gone and brought low; they are taken out of the way as all other, and cut off as the tops of the ears of corn. And if it be not so now, who will make me a liar, and make my speech nothing worth?" (KJV) Hear ye, the Word of God. He does not change.

CHAPTER TWENTY

CLARIFY
THE VISION

W ith the turn of the century, so many things began to happen.
There were some things, however, of which I was sure. It was
clear to me that without vision, the people would perish.

I had resolved to have three locations in New Orleans. I wanted
to meet people where they were. The people came and the Uptown
and East locations were booming. Since there were hundreds of
members coming from the West Bank, we bought a building and renovated it and it quickly became too small. In 1996, we bought thirty
acres on the West Bank and in 1997, we built phase one again.

With one church in three locations, it became necessary to make
ministerial alignments that would make the ministry effective. My
wife became "Co-Pastor."

Prior to Hurricane Katrina, we were attending seven services
each Sunday, covering all three locations. I eventually alternated
preaching some of the services, allowing Debra and Bishop Tommie
Triplett to minister. They were both loved by the congregations and
it allowed me to give due diligence to each service.

The closing of a local naval base enabled us to acquire property which would eventually house more than seventy-five families. We built a senior citizens home, a parent-child care center, and a large commercial facility that housed our corporate headquarters, bringing the administration of our three facilities under one roof. A school building was vacated and Greater St. Stephen acquired the property in 60 days, raising two million dollars to pay for it in cash. The shouting and praises to God that ensued were unimaginable.

As churches in the area became without pastors, there were requests for me to send pastors from our church inventory of clergy to serve in that capacity. My philosophy has always been to send out the best or the cream of the crop. Full Gospel in New Orleans was having such a massive impact on growing churches, it became difficult for me to preach at all of them. If there was an example of the "windows of heaven" pouring out blessings where you wouldn't have room enough to receive them, this was the time. Look at God!

Debra and I had to share even more services. If I personally missed preaching at one, I would make it up the next week. I had to discontinue conducting three-night revivals and tried to take Mondays off after the seven Sunday Services. That didn't always work out. Traveling on Tuesday, back on Wednesday for Bible Study, and out on Thursday and Friday became routine for me. In addition, we were growing our television ministry, which was principally maintained to help Full Gospel go to the next level.

It was a time of growth, but also a time of change.

Full Gospel Baptist Fellowship was creating a "stir" in the Black religious community and in particular within the National Baptist Convention. People who were attending traditional Baptist churches were coming to the conferences and to the Fellowship-connected churches to see what was happening. This trying and testing continued until the president of the National Baptist Convention issued a directive for its member churches to either be National Baptist or Full Gospel. This was a point of decision-making for pastors like me, whose earnest desire was to stay in the National Baptist Convention *and* be part of the Full Gospel Fellowship Movement.

One of the worst things that can happen in ministry is when there is a great move of God and you miss the shift. One of the annual themes of the Full Gospel Baptist Fellowship Conference was "Don't Miss the Shift." We can miss destiny trying to please people. If you are a leader, pray for the people you are leading, that they may have the spirit to follow your leadership. With all that I've encountered, I thank God that He has allowed me to change forward and not become mired in the past.

There was a time in 2000 that I actually grew tired of the work. One of my mentors growing up was Dr. Caesar A. Clark, the eminent senior pastor of Goode Street Baptist in Dallas, Texas. He told me, after hearing me preach when I was in my twenties: "Son, you're a good preacher, but you're going to burn out, because you preach too hard."

My plan was a little different. I was going to give my best and when I couldn't do anymore, I would step down. I had no intention of trying to preserve my preaching energy as a pastor, until I was ninety years old.

I could not help notice that my vision for the future was not as clear to me as it had been. I also knew that where there is no vision, the people perish, and I never wanted to see what God allowed me to build and become, perish. While it was exciting to be able to go from one location to two, and then, to three, I was not excited about creating a fourth. I had built buildings, bought acres of land, and developed programs for future growth, but I had grown tired. Like Paul, I had fought the good fight, but he was preparing for death. I only wanted to prepare for retirement. Anyone who has known me knows that I am a planner and my planning at that time was focused on succession.

I've always believed in retirement, but I don't believe that you should try to pastor beyond your time. I've seen pastors grow their ministries and then stay too long, only to see the ministry die before their eyes.

I had a long talk with God. I had learned early to open myself up to hearing the voice of God and allowing Him to give direction as He had given purpose to my life and my work. I told Him that in ten years, I wanted to retire. I told Him that I didn't want to stop preaching because I wanted to mentor pastors, plant churches, and show pastors the keys to being successful. I saw myself planting churches and placing pastors, like my namesake, Paul. I wanted to teach at our school and enjoy my latter years. I had experienced so much success through the years; I felt I could retire at sixty. I needed to hear from the Lord as it related to that plan because I didn't want to do anything without His approval.

The response that I received from God was the "strangest" that He ever given me since I accepted Him as my personal savior. He said, "If that's what you want to do." I was stunned and became mesmerized in unbelief that God would leave this magnitude of my personal decision up to me. For me, that was the green light because that's what I wanted to do. I loved Greater St. Stephen. I loved and respected the ministry team. They were my faithful and loyal friends, but I knew I was called to begin the transition to retirement.

I planned my announcement to Greater St. Stephen that I was going to pastor ten more years because God had released me and told me that it was left up to me. By this time, many of my creative juices were slowing down and I wanted to leave "on top."

I went to the Fellowship at the July 2000 Conference and shared the same message with them. I had witnessed how God had brought together one of the most powerful movements in the world. The favor of God was on the Fellowship, in the face of other reformations which were at least a hundred years older. I was honored to serve as Presiding Bishop, but I had received permission from God to be released.

I was determined to give all of my final years to Greater St. Stephen and to Full Gospel. I had to end strong so that my last ten years would be my best years. I had influenced and carefully watched as both of these entities grew. Over the years, we had become a strong and caring "family" and that was awesome to see while you are living and in your right mind.

My decision was consistent with the theme of the Fellowship: "Changing a Generation." I had a clear mandate to teach people how to change. In order for change to be effectuated, there had to be vision. At Greater St. Stephen, it was the sixteen steps: Vision of the House. At the Fellowship, it was the *"Full Gospel Distinctives"* and a "Statement of Purpose," which I called the "Right to Choose Statement." Like the vision of Habakkuk, each had to be written and made plain.

Dr. Samuel Chand wrote in his book, *Who's Holding Your Ladder?*, that despite what we might believe, it's not our beautiful churches, neither our dynamic worship, nor the inspired preaching that draws people to houses of worship. Rather, it is vision. All of those things, as well as praise and worship, are components of the vision, but that is not the vision of the twenty-first-century church. It is not a place where we gather to have a "good time." It has to be about person and purpose.

Being balanced was part of the vision. My inspiration had come from three areas, movements, or reformations. The first was from the position of the so-called "Word Church." Recognizing that there was a lack of balance in the African-American Church, these ministries elected to minimize any kind of emotion or feelings in worship and preaching, and to make those things secondary to academics or learning. Many of them went too far to the right to eliminate what they considered "unnecessary emotions."

Learning, in its purest form, requires that you synthesize what you hear and distinguish between what is good and bad. I wanted us to seriously study the word of God by listening and then applying it to life. Faith comes by hearing and hearing by the word of God. There was an apparent need for the Body of Christ to shift and the faith teachers within the Word Churches brought that to the table, and I wanted that. Dr. Fredrick K. C. Price was a great leader in that area and I gained much inspiration from his teachings.

Yet, as a practical matter, inspiration without some attendant or resulting emotion was impractical. When the word is good, you should say something! The time of preachers, who made it their theme to teach that we are supposed to be "broke down here in order to be rich over yonder," was against all that I knew about God. We are not "poor strangers traveling through a barren land."

Coming from the Church of God in Christ, I knew that making a joyful noise unto the Lord was important. I took the jubilation with balance and the tenets of the Word Church, as well. We had to study the word but there had to be feeling. When the word is good, you have to say something. You don't have to scream and holler but you should be able to show some kind of emotion.

Finally, the Baptist church always talked about the death, burial, and resurrection of Jesus Christ. It was foundational in principle. Yet, they did not go far enough in the teaching on the Holy Ghost, the Third Person of the trinity. They had Him included but with "limited power." There was no need to try to get someone to "speak in tongues" and they were not yet saved. We have to take first things first. You can't be filled unless you are saved. You can't make a sinner get filled with the Holy Ghost but you can grow a believer into receiving the Holy Ghost in its fullness. Your mind has to grow and develop so that you will know how to receive the blessings from the Lord.

The Full Gospel of Jesus Christ is never "watered-down to make people feel better." It is the true full word of God. It is complete and preachers have the obligation to bring the whole word of God. If the gospel is going to be full and effective, the one bringing the word must be anointed or set apart by God. You're telling people how to live and living the life yourself.

The President of the United States and members of Congress are held to the highest standards of personal conduct, but there should be an even higher standard of conduct as a priority in the pulpit. The worse thing that can happen to a minister, preacher, or pastor is that he loses his influence. It's important to speak truth, even when people don't like to hear it. People were offended because Jesus spoke the truth. In most cases, the offended people were the "church" or temple people.

There are preachers who don't want to preach against sin anymore because it's offensive. The Bible says, "Know the truth and the truth will make you free." I was shocked when I heard the pastor of a mega church state that he didn't preach about sin or the blood any longer because church people don't want hear about a cross, crucifixion, and the blood. He said he builds his sermons around "love." I had to seize the moment to remind him that the "blood" is "love." Water can't wash away sins; soap can't wash away sins; bleach can't wash away sins. Nothing but the blood of Jesus can do that.

We gleaned from each of these entity positions and created "a mixture" for the Full Gospel Baptist Church Fellowship. We sought and found a "flavor" that was distinctive to Full Gospel.

There has to be a defined destination and purposeful intent in order to retain people in the body of Christ or anywhere else where there is a desire for substance.

Dr. Samuel Chand, whom I admire as a practical thinker, spoke to the issue of "vision," when he suggested that all legitimate visions are "portable." If the vision statement can't fit on a T-shirt, it's probably too long. If we want people to know who we are and what we do, we must transport the vision from place to place. Regardless of where we are, people should be able to know who you are and the principles of faith upon which you stand.

If the job of communicating the vision is done well, anyone who is anywhere, who is part of the attainment of the vision should be able to clearly communicate and explain it to anyone else. It should not be necessary to tell someone to give you time to contact your pastor or the bishop to get an explanation of what you believe and practice in your faith walk. The vision is portable.

I have lived long enough to see a big difference in the Full Gospel Baptist Church Fellowship from the time of its 1994 inception. We have changed a generation and that's what I was called to do. In our eighteenth conference, I asked our youth eighteen and under to stand among the people. Thousands of young people stood who were not even born when Full Gospel started. Now, they are involved in the Fellowship, having never known the struggles, arguments, and contentions about titles and the role of women in leadership.

CHAPTER TWENTY-ONE

C.H.A.N.G.E.

O ur ministry and the Fellowship have always been about
change. I found out, however, that there was need for a shorter
version of the "vision"—one that was more facilitative of those who
would hear, as well as for those who were trying to explain it. It was
important to make sure that every explanation of where we were trying to go was consistent, factual, faithful, and spiritual. We wanted
to be sure we were saying and meaning the same thing.

We developed the acronym of C.H.A.N.G.E. (and it can fit on a
T-shirt). "C" was indicative of being a church of love that was both
Committed and Consistent.

Consider all of the things in which you are involved and ask, *if
everyone were like me, would it be a success?* You must know
how important you are to the kingdom and not minimize that
importance.

I preached a sermon titled "God Plus One," from Judges 7:20.
One part of the text refers to the "sword of the Lord and of Gideon."
I found it strange that the writer of the text should add the name of

Gideon to the name of God. Could the addition of any one person add weight to the name of God. It would seem that the second name weakens the force of the first. Would not the sword of Jehovah have been sufficient? One stroke of His sword would destroy or annihilate any host. Why then, should Gideon's name be added. God needed Gideon because it was literally the army of Gideon, as well as the army of the Lord that gained victory.

There is undeniable importance in "one." Think of things which emphasize the value of "one." One link in a chain. One letter is essential to complete the alphabet and no alphabet can adequately function without all of the letters. The reform of medical nursing was not done by a cooperative association of physicians, but, rather, one woman, Florence Nightingale. Aaron Burr missed being the President of the United States by one vote. By one vote, Andrew Johnson missed impeachment.

The reality of these actualities is missed, however, because it was God plus Gideon. As he mustered an army of 32,000 men, he had a plan for that mass of warriors to deliver Israel, and knowledge of that fact gave him assurance of gratification. The shock came when God told him he had to dismiss some of the men, releasing 22,000 at one time and 9,700 later. What could he do with an army of 300 men against 135,000 enemies?

God wanted Gideon and the rest of us to know that God plus one is the majority. God plus one makes the difference. The admonition to Gideon is the same for us. You are the one that God wants to use. You are the one who is going to help move the church to the next level because He is with you. When you are committed and consistent, you and God can make a big difference.

The "H" in change stands for Holy Ghost Empowered—more of Him and less of you. The "H" is important because that's why God told me to take the people to the next level. We get so wrapped up in what people think that we lose power. Though we live in a different age and a time where people are becoming less committed to what God is saying, we cannot lower the standard in the Body of Christ. Deliverance gets beyond your experience with God, lasting only for a short time. You can become so absorbed by the position that there is no commitment to fight for that in which you believe. But the Holy Ghost is present and calls us to fight, to stand strong, and to grow.

The "A" in change stands for Advancing the Kingdom. The kingdom is God's way of doing things. It is the production in us of a God-like, God-pleasing character. It's all about building the kingdom, not building you. I don't want things to be centered around me. It should be centered around God and represent the kingdom.

The "N" is for Nurturing [building up] and Networking [supporting each other] the vision. There is no need to wait for the downfall of others because you feel you can do the job better. Take the ability and strengths you have and build them up. In our ministry, we have created a business society, where we ask business owners in the church to subscribe to a directory of businesses we have in the ministry. If we have electricians, plumbers, doctors, lawyers, and so forth, we support them because they are in the "family."

The "G" is for God Glorifying Praise and Worship to Him. I believe Full Gospel helped many churches to go to the level where you enter into His gates with thanksgiving and into His courts with praise. It is wonderful to be known as a worshipper; no other title means as much to me.

The "E" indicates the desire to Evangelize and Edify. We are compelled to go into the byways and compel the people to come.

Pastors tend to wait in expectation of gaining new members from those who leave other churches. The fact is that the "recycling program" is strong in the church. The question is how many baptisms are you having each year as a result of people being saved? There are still people who need Jesus. The obligation we have is to go and find them and bring them to know Jesus. The "E" also stands for Edifying. We are told to teach the people to observe all things, whatsoever has been commanded. We scatter to evangelize, and we gather to be edified.

In Galatians 1:3-10, Paul defined the Christian redemption in terms of deliverance from the tyranny of the transient.

Somebody has to renew the fact and make it clear that the church is not a fad. In that text, Paul wrestled with something which is familiar to us called "time spirit." It is the principle that things change with the times. The dominion of the time spirit is real in any and every stage of human progress. We are called to be observant of the "time spirit" in the church. It is subtle and hard to analyze. It is an atmosphere which envelops people until they can search for something new and with the purpose of getting more people. Thus, pastors may decide to stop preaching against sin and allow people to leave church services feeling "good." The need for preaching from the gospel of the Old Bible may be diminished. The time spirit will convey the impression that older preachers are replacing younger preachers and the message of salvation has changed. It is the "time spirit" that makes us carnal, which is enmity against God. Carnality is when you allow the flesh to get into that which is spiritual. Galatians 1:6 says: "I marvel that ye are so soon removed from him that called you into the grace of Christ unto another gospel" (KJV).

How can we allow ourselves to go to another gospel and abandon the gospel that saved us? It is the gospel that has truly saved men. It is a gospel that works.

Perhaps preachers are becoming fearful of preaching the true gospel. That's strange because the better way to avoid the conflict of preaching the gospel of Jesus as opposed to some new faddish version of the "good news," would be to simply declare yourself a "motivational speaker," rather than a preacher. That way you won't have to use the pulpit and you can profane and rant and rave all you want. Those with itching ears will flock to you, celebrating the advent of this "new season."

If the goal is to please men, it is a bad goal. Paul said that if your goal is to "please" men, you are not a servant of Jesus Christ. If your calling is by the revelation of Jesus Christ, then the only legitimate option you have is to follow Him.

Another gospel "time spirit" that tends to influence us is known as the "Age of Aquarius." New Age thinking has consumed those who seek to experience a new openness to one another through nature, and who consider the awareness and acceptance of this thinking as the basis of a universal force. It may be best recognized as the true manifestation of one's self, even if it violates established and accepted morals. It means not to come out of the closet by promoting a "gay church." There would be no need to talk or think negatively about it because it is the Age of Aquarius, which is filled with the open display of love.

The problem is that love without discipline is not love. Love without correction is not love. Love without truth is not love. The love of God declares that regardless of your sins, the blood of Jesus can wash the sins away and make you a new creature according to His word, not another gospel.

Even the apostle, Paul was told that much learning had made him mad. As he began his discourse on the good news of Jesus, the conclusion of those around him was that he had lost his mind. Intellectual blindness is dangerous. Except you place the Spirit over the mind, all of your rational faculties become incapable of conclusions on any spiritual subject. The cultivation of the intellectual parts of man can, of itself, have no tendency toward moral or spiritual good. It may create a generation of philosophical skeptics about virtue, but it cannot produce moral and saved people.

My physician may love his patient, but he cannot say, "I love you so much that I can't tell you about the cancer in you." That would not be real love. A preacher must tell you what's in you and what must come out of you in order for you to have abundant life. He has to tell you when it will destroy you, and admonish you not to live that way. You need to be empowered to take authority over the "time spirit." If God is in the time, it is the *right* time.

CHAPTER TWENTY-TWO

THE RIGHT
TO CHOOSE

For many years, our South African brothers and sisters experienced "Apartheid." It was a system of government as well as a way of life when South African Blacks had the right to be born, but beyond that all other rights were denied because of skin color. They were not allowed to vote, and government positions of authority were reserved for Whites only. Nelson Mandela, a South African leader openly opposed to the system, joined with like-minded others to fight until the rights they now enjoy were achieved. After years of oppression, persecutions, and imprisonments, they now can freely exercise the "Right to Choose" decisions that will ultimately improve their quality of life.

In the same way, the Baptist Church has experienced "Spiritual Apartheid." We have always had the right to be born again, but spiritual gifts, heavenly language, the power to cast out demons, laying on of hands, etc. were afforded to others in the Body of Christ, but were denied to Baptists. We are standing as "spiritual Mandelas," boldly declaring our rights as "Baptists" to make a choice. We can no longer allow the denomination (our governing body) to tell us that we can't have this because "we are Baptists," when Jesus, Who is Head of the Church says, "We can." We have the "Right to Choose" (Mark 16:17-18).

It is not a matter of others in the Baptist church not preaching the gospel fully. The complete gospel is Jesus Christ—His death, burial, and resurrection. We have also stood on the fact that He got up from the grave with all power in His hands. The reason we remain Baptist and support the Baptist church is because of the solid foundation in Jesus Christ.

As Full Gospel Baptists, we do not believe that we have fully used the power that Jesus left when he returned to glory. He left His power with us when He returned. The Bible says, "Whatsoever ye shall loose on earth shall be loosed in heaven" (Matthew 18:18).

God has given us the power to take authority over the enemy, but we are scared. Do you realize that we have the "Keys to the Kingdom?" (Matthew 16:19). These "keys" represent the authority and power to open and to unlock. These are the keys to the kingdom of heaven—the place that has everything—peace, love, healing, prosperity, and protection. Jesus promised to give us the keys to all of this. It was given to us by Jesus and regardless of what happens, you cannot lose the keys.

When my children reached a certain age, my wife allowed me to present the keys of our house to them. I made a big ceremony out of it. With great authority and solemnity, I went into my speech: "I believe you are old enough to get the keys to the Morton household. First, the only reason you are getting the keys is because of our relationship. You are my daughters and son. Our relationship is special. Second, don't get so distracted or busy with your own agenda that you lose the keys, because then some unauthorized person, who has no relationship with us could come in and take everything that is rightly ours—things that your mother and I have worked to achieve. Don't lose your keys."

Similarly, as children of God, we are special. The keys to the kingdom have not been given to just anybody. It is because of our relationship to the Father that we get the keys to the kingdom of heaven. Whatever you do in life, if you know Jesus as your personal savior, He has saved you and you have a right to be in the house, but don't lose your keys.

After my long and well-prepared speech to the children, all three of them, at one time or another, have lost their keys. Of course, I let them into the house, but it provided an opportunity for me to teach a lesson about responsibility and belonging.

What does it look like to the world when you claim to be a child of God, but you have no keys and no authority. When the enemy comes against you like a flood, you need your keys so as not to be afraid because

> The LORD is my light and my salvation;
> Whom shall I fear;
> The LORD is the strength of my life;
> Of whom shall I be afraid? (Psalm 27:1)

You have the power, with your keys, to say "Your kingdom come. Your will be done on earth as it is in heaven" (Matthew 6:10). God gave me the authority to stand, regardless of who was coming against me and regardless of the weapons they tried to use. I had the power in the name of Jesus. I knew I had the authority in the name of Jesus because I always keep my keys.

We have dealt with salvation at Calvary, but we have left out the experience at Pentecost. Full Gospel Baptists are using the keys to take authority over the devil. The word of God declares that we can legally use our gifts in the "Name of Jesus!" It does not matter how strange it may look to the natural man or to our denomination. You have the "Right to Choose!"

God told me to "bridge the gap" between Baptists and Pentecostals—two of the largest denominations in the world. This was our focus.

Why did God say to start this movement? It was not a mere fellowship of friends, because we had plenty of those. It was not just to get people saved; Baptist churches were good at that. The foundation was strong. It was letting Baptists know that they had a right to choose if they wanted to experience the fullness of the Holy Ghost. Even though the Baptist doctrine taught against it and Bible doctrines were for it, there was a need to fight for the rights of believers to have it.

Jesus has empowered us to cast out demons, speak with new tongues, to lay hands on the sick and have them recover. The church has the responsibility of preaching the power that God has for His people, so that souls will be saved and set free. Instead, some of the churches have become social clubs, where we only meet and greet, have a good time, collect dues, and depart to our homes until next week, when we will return and do the same thing.

It is indisputable that if the church was operating under the "world system," many of its leaders would have been fired a long time ago. The world system obligates you to produce and if you fail to produce, you lose your job. People in the church are not producing, because we don't want to hurt someone's feelings. The result is the perpetuation of the "Good Ol' Boys Club" within the ranks of church leadership, rather than the church fulfilling its purpose of demonstrating power.

The kingdom is suffering violence and the body of Christ needs to take authority over the violence with the power of the Holy Ghost. I am convinced that some of us need to get out of these pulpits if we're going to continue in the fear of telling people about the power that the Holy Ghost has given us. How can you call it "God's church," when there are no results? God is taking the church to another level and His power to do that is real.

A lesson to remember is that the Lord is not here to divide His church. The first thing the enemy will say when we begin to preach the fullness of the Holy Ghost is to suggest to congregations and leaders that they are dividing the church.

My assignment was never to divide the church in any way. Denominations have already been pretty successful at that. It is pretty difficult to explain to a rational, thinking person that we are all supposed to be going to the same heaven but we cannot be in fellowship on earth because of denominational differences. It is my desire to expand "Kingdom Power" to those who have a desire to receive something that is biblical: the fullness of the Holy Ghost—more of Him and less of you.

A lesson might be learned from observing the actions of the over-the-air television networks at the advent of cable television. They did not elect to fight the cable networks. Instead, they realized that people were ready for more television option channels. They chose to link with the cable networks in their advertising because it expanded the territory of the networks.

We can learn something from the networks. The Lord is not here to divide His church. The first thing the enemy will say when we begin to preach the fullness of the Holy Ghost is to suggest to congregations and leaders that they are dividing the church.

Please know that some people don't want it, and you don't have to have it. I know plenty of good Baptists who don't speak in tongues but are so close to God in their praying. They are loving people who have raised their children in the fear of God. There is no basis for telling people that because they haven't been filled with the evidence of speaking in tongues that they are not going to heaven. They are! This is a gift, and you don't force a gift on someone. They have to have a desire to take it, if they want it.

It will never be our intent to fight against the body of Christ or Baptists. We believe that the foundation is right and that it is strong. There is more, however, if you want to subscribe. The subscription is free.

The gospel is also right for right now, right here. What if a reputable person left you five million dollars in a will, with the condition that when you turned seventy years old, the five million would be yours. Are you going to wait until you're seventy to begin living? Would you decide that you're not going to work because you will have five million when you turn seventy? Would you go around begging until your age changed? The answer should be an emphatic "No!" Most of us would let seventy take care of itself. You have to live right now. You have to survive right now.

That's what the Holy Ghost is all about. Heaven is secured. You're going to heaven when you die. What about now? The devil is stomping all over you right now and you're talking about it being "all right after while, by and by." God has more for us right now and God will give you more to come against the attacks of the enemy, now.

Our daughters are being raped and our sons are being murdered. The devil is continuously destroying marriages. Racism is at its highest, and recession has perverted relationships. There are wars and rumors of wars. When you are having that kind of trouble, you need power. The power that you need is from the Holy Ghost because the devil is stronger than you, when you fight in the flesh. You need to be built-up in the Holy Ghost.

We have to halt trying to change the "flavor of the gospel" as if it were our own. We have to refrain from sugarcoating the word so that people won't be afraid of the power of Jesus. "And these signs shall follow them that believe. In my name shall they cast out devils; they shall speak with new tongues; . . . they shall lay hands on the sick, and they shall recover" (Mark 16:17-18 KJV).

First Corinthians 14 admonishes us to follow after charity or "love" and to desire spiritual gifts "but rather that ye may prophesy. When speaking in "tongues," you have to understand to whom you are speaking. You are not speaking to men, but to God. No person understands the one who speaks in tongues unless they have the gift of interpretation. If all I did was speak in tongues, I would be no good as a preacher because no one would understand it.

It would be as if you were in a foreign country and could not understand the language of the locals. When I am in France, I don't get upset when the people around me are speaking French. If, however, they are talking to me, I would need an interpreter. "He that speaks in an unknown tongue edifies himself, but he that prophesies, edifies the church" (1 Corinthians 14:4).

On the other hand, if by the Spirit I prophesy, which means I speak with understanding, the church would then be edified. Speaking in tongues all of the time is not spiritual; it is foolish. Yet, to speak in your heavenly language is to build you up or edify you.

151

This is not something I heard or something I read about. I am a living witness to what speaking in your heavenly language can do for you.

Being filled with the Holy Ghost is not merely speaking in tongues. It is about the power to live right. I awaken in the morning speaking in tongues. When I am preparing my sermonic messages, I speak in tongues because I need to be edified in my spirit. Even after these many years of preaching, there are still some reservations of the responsibility of preaching a word that could save a person's life or at the very least, give them enough faith to walk into their new destiny. That's a serious matter and I don't take it lightly. I need the Lord to help me. I don't need the people to see me; I want them to see the anointing on my life. The best way I can do that is to move me out of the way.

The devil tries to cheat us. He wants to keep the church off balance. He wants the church to be where they don't receive anything from God. When you are strengthened and lifted up in the Spirit, the devil has no foothold.

Praying in tongues is praying from your spirit, instead of from your intellect. There are two ways you can pray: (1) in the Spirit, or (2) with your mind; with your understanding. Both are correct and effective. When you pray with your mind, you pray with your understanding, but you can only go so far. Regardless of how brilliant you are, you will only get as much as you know. Speaking in tongues means that the spirit of God is beginning to move through you. The language of the Spirit goes beyond your intellect. When the Holy Spirit, Who lives within you, desires to speak, He knows exactly how to say it (Romans 8:26).

When I was at home in Canada, I was praying the wrong prayer: "Lord, I just want to work here in my city for you. Help me in my city to make an impact." When I began to speak in the Spirit, the Spirit began to speak to me and said, "Move to New Orleans." I did not understand that with my mind because Mortons didn't move, but that is what He intended for me.

In addition to relocation, there was a big struggle to change to Baptist. This would require a miracle, but God said, "Do it." Trying to "un-learn" what I had been taught all of my life took a special anointing that resulted in my changing forward. Anyone can keep the status quo, but can you dare to be different when you know you are on an assignment?

Philippians 3:13-14 is clear when it says: "Brethren, I count not myself to have apprehended: but this one thing I do, forgetting those things which are behind, and reaching forth unto those things which are before, I press toward the mark for the prize of the high calling of God in Christ Jesus" (KJV).

The conquering phrase is "this one thing I do." The difference between an amateur and a professional is that the amateur pursues what he does when it is convenient, while the professional makes it his life's business. They are amateur Christians who pursue the Christian life when they feel like it. Well, if you want to be a Christian after God's heart, you must make His business your business, giving it the same attention, concentration, and unwavering energy as you do the things you cherish the most.

When you are singularly focused, people will call you a fanatic, but you can't worry about that. Whatever I do, I want to do it all to the glory of God. That's the "mark." Paul tells us to pursue this aim with "forgetfulness"—forgetting those things which are behind. The art of forgetting has much to do with the success and power of everyday life. His analogy was of an athletic runner, who had no time to focus on the mark that he had already run.

What should I forget? Forget failures that paralyze your hopes and dreams. There is no place in your past that is so bad that you cannot be victorious going forward. Never let the past limit your hopes of possibilities. Stay focused. If you have tried something so often and failed, don't conclude that it's not worth trying again. We have to remember Paul's exhortation to forget those things which are behind and press toward the mark.

I saw that there were those who were going to fight against me no matter what I did. Anything I did was wrong as far as some were concerned. Changing forward, I was already accepted in other denominations, with no problem, but I wanted to bring the title of Bishop to the Baptist Church.

I needed us to use biblical times as our reference point. Instead of calling the leader of our movement "Mr. President," like the leader of the United States Government, I said for us to use the biblical name "Bishop."

The Lord had said for me to be a "pastor's pastor." These ministries needed to grow and be blessed and my assignment was to provide mentorship by taking them under my wing. The church needed to go back to God's way, realizing that His people are peculiar, set apart, and different. I was to gather pastors to show them what God was doing. God has allowed me to be a successful example for others. I had been a successful pastor, so I could be a successful bishop, leading others. That's what God called me to do.

Always, in creating Full Gospel, the question must be, "Is this what God wants?" We had to make changes and that created resistance in some areas. Some were determined not to change, but we were committed to change forward.

Leaders must change and with that comes new ways of doing things. My wife is now senior pastor of the church where I served as senior pastor for more than thirty-three years. I am still living, but God told me to appoint her there, not as a "maintenance pastor" to continue what I did, but to be creative and unafraid to change things and people that needed changing. Things that worked for me may not have worked for her. We must serve this generation. I am called as an agent of change for this generation.

Because we have reverenced our forefathers over God, the result has been confusion. The confusion is not the fault of God. He is not in confusion and He is not the author of "confusion." The assurance that there is no confusion in God's church is when there is adherence and obedience to His word. In bringing about Full Gospel Fellowship, I was told by others to "leave it alone." The problem is that we leave too much "alone" trying to please everyone and make them happy. We can't change a generation by leaving things alone. It would create even more confusion. Through FOCUS and prayer, we are changing forward for and with a new generation.

CHAPTER TWENTY-THREE

THE CONTENTION OVER WOMEN IN MINISTRY

There were three major struggles that we had in establishing Full Gospel: the Holy Ghost, Bishops, and the role of women in church leadership. First Corinthians 14:34 says: "Let your women keep silence in the churches: for it is not permitted unto them to speak; but they are commanded to be under obedience, as also saith the law" (KJV).

It is amazing how many people play God and do what they want to do whenever it suits them. The pastor, then, becomes "God" and declares that women must keep silent in the church, but you can sing in the choir. If he really believed that women should be silent in the church, perhaps he should have an "all male chorus" and nothing else. Preaching is proclaiming the good news of Jesus Christ. Whether you sing "The Lord Will Make a Way Somehow" or if you talk it, you are proclaiming the Good News of Jesus Christ and that is preaching. Instead, we apply the rules where we want. That's why we have to break up in our churches the spiritual Afghanistans, Irans, and Iraqs, where the women keep their faces covered and where they must be quiet and treated like second-class citizens, because the leader does not know the word of God.

In the Bible, the place of men seems more pronounced in the number who filled leadership positions. Yet, I find that the Bible places no restrictions of women of God ministering. The apostle, Paul, who told women to be silent in the church said in Romans 16:1: "I commend unto you Phoebe our sister, which is a servant of the church which is at Cenchrea" (KJV).

She worked in the church and was commended by Paul for her work. He went on to call for the assistance of others to her needs and identified himself as her spiritual covering. Paul was not against women preachers. Further, in Philippians 4:3, Paul encouraged others to the women who had labored with him in getting people coming to the Lord.

The acceptance of women in a public place of ministry in the church is not a concession to the spirit of the Feminist Movement. These women were and are Holy Ghost–filled women, and the Bible says that "in the last days," God will pour out His Spirit on men and women.

In the last days, God is using men and women. The Lord has anointed women, and many of them to stand up and some of the men sit down. Conceding to male chauvinism would be allowing the flesh to get into that which is spiritual.

My wife is an anointed woman of God and has served as my co-pastor since the early 1990s. People talked about it endlessly, saying that the church had two heads and anything with two heads was a "freak." I guess it's about as freakish as a pilot and copilot. The fact of the matter is that there is no confusion between the pilot and copilot because the copilot always submits to the pilot. The prefix "co" stands for "co-op," as in cooperation or agreement. They are in singular accord to fly the airplane.

I needed someone to help me "fly the plane." If Greater St. Stephen had been a "small plane," everything would have been fine, but when it grew into a 747, I needed a co-pastor. She helped me in so many areas, and the arrangement became a perfect fit.

Caution must be taken, however, because "co-pastor" can become a fad in churches. Just because the husband is a pastor does not mean that the wife automatically becomes the "co-pastor." My wife and I have a special connection and understanding. She knows that I take the lead and there is no confusion over that. Her role is just as important.

In fact, my brother Bishop C. L. Morton was my co-pastor before Debra. My wife never became upset over that and submitted to my spiritual authority. In our church, we have female elders, ministers, deacons, and women in other leadership positions. In Full Gospel, we have Bishops, overseers, and pastors, who are female and leading—all of them submitting to our covering which is the order of God. It's biblical.

We have had turmoil and confusion because of a lack of knowledge. When men and women went to the first-century church, they did not sit together. The men sat on one side and the women on the other because the men were to be the spiritual heads of their households and their entire focus was on the word of God. Too often, women are the spiritual heads of the home and the men don't know anything about the word of God. God designed the man to take the spiritual reins at home. In fact, verse 35 says, "and if they will learn any thing, let them ask their husbands at home: for it is a shame for women to speak in the church" (KJV).

The husband should be able to teach and share the word with his family.

Paul was preaching a sermon that is as controversial today as it was then. He could not help but hear all of the commotion: "How could that be?" "Paul is off track on that." It is no doubt that it was at that point that he was compelled to say, "Be quiet. There's too much confusion." Perhaps, the women were trying to strain and get the attention of their husbands on the other side of the room and became a distraction for those trying to listen to Paul's sermon. I don't find that scenario unusual because my wife and I go through that each time we attend a service where someone else is preaching. She will get a revelation from what they are saying and insist on telling me about it while I'm trying to get my own revelation. I can identify with Paul.

The whole point of Paul's addressing the women in the first place was the matter of confusion. He was talking about undisciplined discussion that was disturbing the service. There are several scriptures that teach what women should do in the church. They were speaking and ministering in the church, even during Paul's time. The writer Luke, in Acts 2:17-18, repeats the sayings of the prophet, Joel in declaring that the handmaidens shall prophesy, which means "preach with understanding." It is proclaiming the good news of Jesus Christ. In Acts 21:9, Philip, the evangelist, had four daughters, who prophesied. Women preached the word of God.

I'm sure there are those who would rather have men who aren't living "the life" preach to them but will refuse to listen to a Holy Ghost–filled woman, who has the Word in her spirit, who is saved and sanctified, and filled with the Holy Ghost

In many cases, we have broken the chauvinistic spirit, especially in the Full Gospel Baptist Church Fellowship. The question is and always has been: Will we adhere to God's Laws or Social Laws? If we consider the language in 1 Corinthians 11:5-7, people are being disobedient to God. The passage deals with the uncovered heads of women and covered heads of men. There are many women who do not cover their heads and as many men who wear their hair long. Does that mean that either is more or less spiritual? Paul took great pains to distinguish those things that he said were spiritual and those that were based upon his best opinion. He would let his readers know the difference in the application of a passage based upon the word of God and that which was subjective to him.

With that said, the churches of God don't have to abide by this particular rule about head covering (1 Corinthians 11:16). Based upon this passage, if you find any division or strife, the word is null and void. The fact of the matter was that Paul's reference as to covering had to do with the woman's submissiveness to her husband and not the physical covering. It had to do with the respect that was engaged in the marital relationship. Women who appeared publicly bareheaded in that culture were considered "loose" and "immoral." He represented the behavior of the prostitutes, who showed no submission to any man. Their heads were uncovered. The behavior was a public disgrace at that time in that culture.

It is clear that the matter of the head of a woman being covered in public to show submissiveness is not a contemporary behavior.

God deals with the total man. There are certain things in the Bible that have only a physical application; there are others that are only spiritual. When you operate in the spiritual, there is not going to be any conflict if you are in the will of God. The physical comes under the spiritual. Following 1 Corinthians 11, many of the Corinthian women wanted sexual equality with the men based on the statement that there is no difference for men and women in the benefits in Christ. Accordingly, Paul writes in Galatians 3:28: "There is neither

Jew nor Greek, there is neither bond nor free, there is neither male nor female: for ye are all one in Christ Jesus" (KJV).

What category would you put this scripture: physical or spiritual? It is spiritual and has nothing to do with the physical. There is neither male nor female in Christ Jesus.

Women of God need and must have a covering. Thus, a woman shouldn't get up when she is ready to minister and say, "Oh, no! There is nobody over me now but Jesus." Then, she might remove her wedding ring to preach. That's not good, nor is it in order. Put on the wedding ring because when you are ministering, you do so spiritually, but you are still in the physical. That's why the Bible reminds us that we worship God in Spirit and Truth. You are still married and still under authority.

All of us are under authority. Whether married or single, you need a spiritual covering. If you are married, however, the word of God will let you know that you need this physical covering. If a married woman of God has received a word from the Lord to speak, she should proceed with all vigor, but if her husband says "No," she might need to sit and reason it out with her husband.

God says that the husband must listen to God, but the wife must listen to the husband. Some husbands, unfortunately, are not listening to God, but they still want to tell wives what to do. They find "comfort" in Ephesians 5:23-25. Yet, women and husbands need to understand that there are some things that wives don't have to obey. A husband could tell his wife that he loves her but because the family is broke, he wants his wife to obey him and become a prostitute in order to get the family some money. The Scripture has never called for obedience to something that is not in the will of God for your life.

We are called upon to obey God's law and the law of the land.

If a "serious husband" has a wife in ministry, and he tells her that she is going too much and needs to slow down and take care of responsibilities at home, she has an obligation to her husband and family. She should not think that he is stupid for desiring to have his wife with the family. Submission is important. In our marriage, my wife teaches and preaches the word of God with power. When I get an invitation to preach in New York or Detroit, I always tell them that I have to check my calendar and check with my "executive assistant" to see if that is a good date. Then, I can tell them of my acceptance.

On the other hand, when they would call my wife with an invitation to preach, especially when the children were growing up, she would always check to make sure it was all right with me, as her husband and her covering.

In our marriage, I also make sure I don't exclude the scripture that refers to "due benevolence," which means mutual respect. Husbands and wives must respect each other.

There have been times when I was ready to book an invitation and she reminded me that it would interfere with the family vacation or something we were supposed to do with the children together. I had to change that date because she is my helpmeet and I respect her. This is not an ego trip because I am a man. I listen to God and this is the spiritual side of me.

There are many people who don't like to submit nor be accountable. They will put on the air of humility but they really are not.

God will change the world with humble people. The meek shall inherit the earth. Second Chronicles 7:14 says, "If my people, which are called by my name, shall humble themselves, and pray, and seek my face, and turn from their wicked ways; then will I hear from heaven, and will forgive their sin, and will heal their land" (KJV).

I believe God has allowed me to cover so many people because humility is the key.

CHAPTER TWENTY-FOUR

THE DAY THAT CHANGED MY DESTINY

After moving to New Orleans in 1972, I learned quickly that I had to get used to hurricanes. Out of all of the hurricanes that hit the city prior to August 29, 2005, I never left the city because of one until Hurricane Katrina. God would always give me peace. But Katrina was a storm like no other.

Whenever a storm was approaching, the news outlets would continue to inform of us of the mayor's evacuation announcements. We remained at home through most of them depending on the category of the storms. I even joked about my parishioners asking me about whether to leave rather than relying on the television news. If I didn't evacuate, then it meant everything was going to be all right. Evacuating was expensive. For Hurricane Katrina, God had to really speak to me.

Late on Saturday night, before Katrina hit, God told me to prepare to leave after church on Sunday. I told my wife that we were leaving. For once, she wanted to stay instead of me. We had just built our "dream house" and had been in it less than a year. Also, she was now pastor of Changing a Generation Arabi and she wanted to stay to lead and support them.

Her pastoral spirit wanted to stay, but as her covering, I said no. This was the first time God had told me to leave New Orleans for a storm, so the plan was to leave that Sunday afternoon. Although many people had already left, we had services Sunday morning in all our locations with Debra and me leading the East locations.

As I was beginning to start the second service at the East location, the city issued a mandatory evacuation. I encouraged everyone to obey and to leave. We made telephone calls to people who were not at church or who might not know about the order to make sure that everyone got out. I told everyone that we would see them on the next Sunday because hurricanes always blew over. The same word was given to all of our members at each location by our assistants.

I was already scheduled to preach in New Jersey on Tuesday night, so, with the church plane, we flew there. I had no idea that this would be the last Sunday that I would see New Orleans in the way I had known it. Arriving in New Jersey, it was all over the television at the hotel about Hurricane Katrina and the expectations of it getting worse.

Everyone knows what happened next.

The cameras' views over CNN showed many of the streets with which I was familiar, including Read Boulevard, where our largest church location was, under water with only the roof showing. I could recognize it because it was next to a high-rise Methodist Hospital. So much pain filled my heart.

For the first time since I was sixteen, I didn't want to preach. I asked my wife to call the church in New Jersey and tell them that I couldn't go. Because she is a spiritual woman, she reminded me that we could not give the enemy the victory and that we could not let the storm stop us from doing what God had called us to do. I began to change forward. I knew the kingdom was suffering violence and I knew that I had to take it back by force. God knew that I needed this assurance from Him and the power of God manifested in a mighty way.

On a personal note, I had to ask: how do you start all over at age fifty-five? If I were in my twenties, thirties, or forties, it would be no problem. I could see myself regrouping, but I was fifty-five years old. I prayed on my knees in the room of that New Jersey hotel and said, "Lord, I have been faithful and I have been a leader of integrity. I've tried to do the right thing. How could it end this way for me? I remember clearly what God asked me. "Paul, do you trust me?" I responded, "Lord, You know I trust You." He asked me again: "Do you really trust me?" I said, "Yes, Lord. You have always been there for me through the good and the bad." "Paul, I am going to make your latter greater than your former . . . and you have no time to waste."

Changing forward, you cannot panic. Instead, you have to be patient and listen to His voice clearly. You would have to know my heart for my people to understand where I was coming from in this dialogue with Him.

I was being called by the national television networks to talk about the New Orleans devastation and how I had traveled across the country trying to encourage the scattered people. I had to do something. Most people had moved to Houston, so we went there.

CNN was following me everywhere I went, but I was not interested in photo ops. I was concerned about helping my New Orleans people. It went beyond the members of Greater St. Stephen because I had become a "spiritual father" to the city. I felt their pains. It was like losing your child in a flood and people, seemingly dismissing the tragedy of the moment, were calling for you to smile before a plethora of cameras.

We went to the Astrodome in Houston. I could see the pain of thousands of devastated people, who had literally lost everything. I couldn't make my way through the hordes of people who only wanted to see a familiar face. When the CNN news crew saw the people grabbing and holding me and crying out for me to pray for them, they commented that they didn't know who I was but that the people certainly did. People were running out of the bleachers when they discovered it was me. I stood and listened to many stories and it took hours to get through the crowd where I could talk to everybody. When they announced, "Bishop Paul Morton is here!" the entire Dome went up in a roar! I talked and shared with them a message of hope because I knew that the worst thing that could happen to a people is to lose hope. I knew, because I had lost all of my worldly possessions, but when I saw those people, I forgot all about my losses and began to pray for them.

After that prayer, many in the crowd began to scream out for me to sing, "God's Going to Wipe All Tears Away." This was a song that I had previously recorded and it had lyrics that, in many ways, spoke to the conditions in which we all found ourselves. It was a song of hope. Without any instruments, I began to sing and the Astrodome began to rock and sway with people praising God. We had church! It was an unforgettable experience.

Then we tried to make it back to New Orleans. Baton Rouge was as close as we could get to the city. We went to the Centro-Plex, a large convention center that had been converted to a holding center for those who had been moved from New Orleans, and just as in Houston, we prayed and worshipped with all who were there.

Though I had been told we couldn't get into New Orleans, I saw that the I-10 Interstate was clear in some areas and I proceeded to enter the city.

When I arrived at my exit, some police officers from Chicago were patrolling the city, and all of the exits were blocked. I told them who I was and my reason for being there, but they turned me away.

That night, God awakened me in the middle of the night, telling me to use what I had. I had always been grateful for favor, but I had never taken advantage of it. Two years earlier, the Chief of Police in New Orleans had made me an honorary "Police Lieutenant" and had given me a badge. I took my badge back to New Orleans and went back to the same exit where the same police officer was standing. I showed my badge and told him that I needed to go through. He remembered me from the day before and asked why I didn't show him that in the first place. Then he waved me through.

While I was there, the Chief of Police called me to pray for him. I shared with him and prayed, and he arranged for me to have an Army truck assigned to me as long as I needed it. Wow! God is so awesome.

I took Bishop Brister and a few others with me, and what I found was more devastation than the television could show. Debra and I had lost everything, but that was nothing compared to what we found at our church.

The soldiers drove us over to the East church and my heart broke. By then, the water had somewhat receded from the high mark, but to see pews floating in the water and the podium from which I had preached floating in what used to be aisles was too much for me. I broke down. It had been a place of hope for so many and now all of that was gone. I saw a dead city that once had been vibrant and alive. I saw a church building that was the place of salvation for thousands, now "dead."

On the news, interviews had people declaring that New Orleans would never come back. Hearing that, I cried. God was asking, "Can this city live again? Can this church live again?" I said to myself, "O Lord God, You know. Please give us one more chance." I knew, and I had heard what people were saying about how it was over for New Orleans, but God gave me a peace in my spirit.

God was telling me that he was going to use New Orleans as a living testimony and that when everybody was thinking it was over, God was going to raise us up.

"And will put My Spirit in you, and you shall live, and I will place you in your own land [I'm going to bring both New Orleans and Greater St. Stephen back]. Then you shall know that I, the LORD, have spoken it and performed it, says the LORD" (Ezekiel 37:14). God did restore Greater St. Stephen, although several thousand of our members relocated. It is spiritually stronger now than it was before the storm. With over half of the city returned, it's a new season. People who played with God, pre-Katrina, are now serious. The bones were living.

We were able to meet with New Orleans city leaders in Baton Rouge to discuss saving our city. My thoughts, however, were focused on the Greater St. Stephen "family." They were like sheep, wandering without a shepherd. Many of them were in Houston, Baton Rouge, and Atlanta. We networked with Bishop Dalton Glen in Houston to have church on Saturday evenings, and with Pastor Johnson, who was not part of Full Gospel, but who opened his doors every Sunday morning in Baton Rouge, Louisiana. My brother Bishop James Morton allowed us to use his Atlanta church every Sunday at three p.m.

I didn't really know what God wanted me to do. At the time, I was also trying to do services in Memphis on Monday nights, Dallas on Tuesday nights, literally, trying to have church somewhere every night of the week and on Sundays. Finally, the Holy Ghost, speaking through my wife, admonished me to guard my heart, but not to kill myself. The reality was that by trying to help everybody, I was losing the strength to help anybody.

I listened and we changed our focus to Baton Rouge, Houston, and Atlanta. I thank God for the body of Christ. Pastors were calling me all over the country to preach and to do an offering for me. They knew the church had insurance but they wanted to make sure that all of our needs were met. At every church where we went, people from Greater St. Stephen or New Orleans were in the audience. The churches set up rooms for us to have prayer with the people who were there. It was difficult and heartbreaking, but I encouraged them to trust God.

People from all over the country were sending money, some of it earmarked "For the Bishop Only." I was fine because God had supplied my needs. I had good insurance. I was concerned about rebuilding.

Full Gospel took the forefront by setting up emergency stations in different parts of the country, feeding the hungry and providing clothes and shelter. We supported other churches and ministries.

I knew I was not going to be able to keep up the pace of traveling and ministering, but I waited for God to show me where to settle. Both Houston and Baton Rouge were possibilities because so many of our people were now there, but God said no to both. He told me, "I want you to establish a church in Atlanta."

We held services at my brother's church in the afternoons, and people were joining every week. We commenced services in

October, and by November, the City of New Orleans raised the call for our return. People began to ask whether I was returning, but I had to tell them that the word I had from God was to remain in Atlanta. It occurred to all of us that we had become "one church in two states."

We had three locations in New Orleans. The West Bank location had the least damage and could seat about one thousand, so we made the needed repairs, and on the Sunday we announced the service, it was packed to the point that we had to hold two services. We found that some of the members' homes had not encountered as much damage and they were able to move back into their homes. In addition, there were other churches and their pastors who either had chosen not to return or were unable to do so, and their members became part of our membership. With the insurance monies from the East location, we paid off all of the properties to the point that we were debt-free. We opened the Uptown location as soon as possible, and I began having early morning services at that location and three p.m. services in Atlanta.

My brother and the New Beginning family had been so kind to us, but we didn't want to wear out our welcome. A Realtor, whom I had known from Windsor, had moved to Atlanta and set up business there for a number of years. I encouraged her to begin looking for a site for the Atlanta location. The Realtor located an old Kroger building on Snapfinger Woods in Decatur, Georgia. It was in bad shape, but God was saying that this was the place. We had received an estimate of 1.3 million dollars to make that building usable. Having not spent the money that people had been giving me from around the country, we had saved about $800,000, which was enough to get started but that still made us about $500,000 short.

We couldn't borrow the amount we needed because we were just starting in Atlanta and the lenders wanted at least three years' financial history. They wouldn't accept what we had done in New Orleans. I couldn't ask the Atlanta membership for more because we were raising money to get everything we needed to go into the church. We had only been there for two months and we started with nothing. We could have cut corners, but I firmly believe that anything you build for the Lord should represent the kingdom. I refused to slap a little paint on the walls and call it Greater St. Stephen, Atlanta.

Movie producer, director, writer, and actor Tyler Perry had been a member of Greater St. Stephen in New Orleans several years earlier before he moved to Atlanta. Even with his success, he had never forgotten his home church. I called him one day because he was always checking to see how we were doing. I told him we had found a place, but with him being familiar with real estate, I asked him to visit the location and advise me on how he liked it. He picked my wife and me up and drove over to the site. He liked it and asked me how much it would take to renovate it. I told him the amount that it would take and let him know that we were $500,000 short. Standing there in the shell of that building, Tyler took out his checkbook and wrote a check in the amount of $500,000, causing us to again, be debt-free. That was confirmation for me that God was in the plan.

With the service times as they were, I knew it was going to be difficult to maintain that kind of schedule with a spirit of excellence. I turned the West Bank location over to one of my spiritual sons Bishop Tommie Triplett. The church of which he was pastor before Hurricane Katrina was already worshiping at the West Bank location because their church, Divine Providence, had been severely damaged. He then could have two services: one for Divine Providence and the other for Greater St. Stephen.

Some people will never understand that there are those who actually hear from God and listen to His voice, but that has been the basis of my success as a pastor for over thirty years Any kind of separation hurts, but it was the right thing to do as it relates to New Orleans and Atlanta.

It was not long before the Atlanta church had to move to two services. I never wanted to be a part-time pastor. If I was going to be their pastor, I had to be there. A pastor not only preaches but he guides, protects, and watches over the sheep. Atlanta was the "baby church." I felt I had to be at Greater St. Stephen in Atlanta if they were going to be the best they could be and operate in excellence like Greater St. Stephen in New Orleans.

My wife would go to Greater St. Stephen in New Orleans and preach every first Sunday morning. I would preach the Lord's Supper every first Sunday night. I would go to New Orleans on the third Sunday to preach and my wife would preach in Atlanta every second Sunday morning. They loved my wife in Atlanta and on the fourth Sunday, Bishop Lester Love would leave his church and preach for us. The month was complete as it related to preaching. I also did the Word Explosion [Bible Study] in New Orleans each Thursday night.

I knew that God wanted me to stay connected with Greater St. Stephen, New Orleans, but I also knew that I could not forsake my new assignment by God in Atlanta. I couldn't allow the "baby church" to have a "part-time pastor" either. I had promised Greater St. Stephen that I would never leave them and after so many years, I would keep my word.

One day, I told the Lord that if only I was two people, everything would be fine. That's when God said, "You are two people. You and your wife are one, but two people." Honestly, I didn't want to hear that because I always wanted Debra to be with me, and I knew that what God was telling me would require an extreme sacrifice. I knew Debra's leadership qualities and whatever she does is done seriously. I knew she was more than qualified, and that we had a solid marriage. If God could give His only Begotten Son, I could give Greater St. Stephen my best.

We talked and prayed about it because we enjoyed being at the same place at the same time. We had always worked together as a team in the same city. We discussed the probability of waking up in different cities and having to schedule time together. She finally accepted the appointment to go to Greater St. Stephen as senior pastor.

In meeting with the church leadership as well as the membership, many of them didn't believe me, assuming that I was trying to "ease" my way out of New Orleans, altogether. In reality, it would have been difficult to try and replicate in New Orleans what had taken thirty years to establish, but it could be done being "one church in two states."

When we announced that Debra would now be the senior pastor, hundreds of people in the auditorium stood up and began to clap enthusiastically and were almost as vocal as they were when I was selected as pastor. It was clear. The message had been understood. She would be senior pastor in New Orleans and my co-pastor in Atlanta. I would serve as her co-pastor in New Orleans. Both churches, then, would have successful pastors and leadership.

CHAPTER TWENTY-FIVE

CHANGING THE WAY WE DO CHURCH

God has given me a fresh anointing, a renewed mind, and renewed strength. Now, however, I feel like a new man. With the birth of the new church I no longer felt called to retire at sixty. On my sixty-fifth birthday, I plan to pass the mantle of Full Gospel and remain senior pastor at Changing a Generation Atlanta and co-pastor at Greater St. Stephen New Orleans until my seventieth birthday. Both God and I agree that this will be enough.

I have spent almost my whole life as a pastor I'm in better shape than some young men. My wife objects to that routine of strict diet, daily exercise, and running five miles a day, but I'm fighting old age as hard as I can. I want to show other pastors that they can be just as good in their sixties as they were in their thirties or forties, if they bring their bodies under subjection.

I have time to mentor others. It is important in the African-American church to pass it on. Pastors must listen to God and listen to their congregations and heed the signs when there is no growth.

I thought everything was going great in New Orleans, but things seemed to be going too well. I left everything in God's hands. I knew the devil really hated me, but I was standing on the promises of God. We made it through Hurricane Katrina and losing our grandbaby. I had made it through a breakdown. I had begun to feel like a modern day job. I was truly making my latter greater than my former, but then, something happened.

When I turned fifty, my wife pushed me to have a colonoscopy, but I always put her off.

Until this, Debra had nagged me to do something, but she never "made" me. It was not her personality. That year, however, I know it was God. For the first time in our marriage, Debra went behind my back and had my executive assistant block off a date for me to have a colonoscopy. It was really the Holy Ghost speaking through my wife because she had a boldness that I had never seen in her before.

Her actions were also confirmations of prophecies that I had received a year earlier. I was walking through the halls and a prophet approached me and said that the Lord had told her to tell me that there was a cancer growing inside of my stomach, but that I would live and not die. I received what she said with a courteous and respectful, "God bless you."

A second prophet came to our church attending a prophetic conference. He approached me and said, "Bishop, I hope I am not out of order, but have you been having trouble with your stomach lately?" I said, "No." He said, "Whatever it is, I see it gone." Now, there were two prophecies that addressed the same thing and both saying that I would live and not die.

People with the gift of prophecy must be very careful and give the whole thing to the target of the prophecy. Don't ever be afraid to tell them the truth of what God has shown you.

I kept the appointment and went to the hospital. When I woke from the test I was later looking into the eyes of my doctor and friend. I noticed that his eyes were watery as he stood by my bed. He began to tell me that he had found the cancer. He had tried to remove the cancer but could not remove it all. He said that if I had waited any longer, the cancer would have broken through the wall and spread over my body. It would have been too late. We had to operate and he wouldn't know until after the operation whether I would need chemotherapy. I knew God had used my wife.

I turned to him and declared that I was healed in Jesus' name because I had a promise from God after Katrina that He would make my latter greater than my former.

I preached a sermon entitled, "Who Will Control Your Reality?" from Revelation 12:7-8: "And there was war in heaven; Michael and his angels fought against the dragon, and the dragon fought and his angels, and prevailed not; neither was their place found any more in heaven" (KJV).

What is reality? It is defined by Webster as "that which is authentic, genuine, and true." Yet, reality in this context, is deeper than that. It is rooted in our feelings, attitudes, and beliefs, whether they are right or wrong. Our perception controls and influences our reality. "As [a man] thinketh in his heart, so is he" (Proverbs 23:7).

There is a war going on in you. The spirit is at war with your mind, and your mind is at war with your spirit over who will control your reality. God is real, but so is Satan. Money is real but so is poverty. Healing is real but so is sickness. If each of these is real, the question remains as to who will control your reality.

Who you allow to reign becomes ruler of your reality. Satan works from the spirit realm to control and corrupt your mind through illusions built from carnal desires and fears. Because he is the "father of deceit," he wants you to believe that this world, as it is, is the only world in which we can live. He promotes this world as full of pain, sickness, and poverty and as something with which we have to live.

The truth is that God has established His kingdom, and His word represents actual reality. It is not a myth. It is not a figment of my imagination. It is actual reality.

The reality is that Jesus has given us authority over all of Satan's power. Luke 10:19: "Nothing shall hurt us."

Jesus came to destroy the works of the devil; therefore, we have been set free. Faith in the word makes you free. Each time that you speak your faith, you are establishing your freedom as true reality.

That's what I did with my cancer. I took the word of God and said:

> He was wounded for our transgressions,
> . . . . ;
> The chastisement for our peace was upon Him,
> And by His stripes, we are healed. (Isaiah 53:5)

The word was more real than the cancer. The word is what controlled my reality as I spoke healing to my body.

It is so interesting that the devil tried to convince me to wait until after the conference that year before having the surgery, in case I got some bad news. In that context, I could have "enjoyed" the conference with no distractions or anxieties. I made up in my mind that the devil would not control my reality. I was healed and I'm still cancer free and it's all to God that the glory goes. That's why on the CD that Kurt Carr produced for me, it was important that we sing the song "I'm Still Standing." It was nothing but the grace of God.

About midnight on the first Sunday night of July 2008, we received a call that the Uptown church, our original location, was burning down. We had just completed our Lord's Supper Service earlier that evening, and the church had been filled to capacity. Arriving at the location, we thought it didn't look too bad; but the inside was gutted. Investigations showed that faulty wiring had caused of the fire.

Immediately, some people began to say that we had burned the church down ourselves. Only the official fire investigation put those lies to rest.

Greater St. Stephen, as a church, had been nothing but a positive force in a city that had gained its fame from Bourbon Street and Mardi Gras. It was a major church that was changing a generation. How God could take me and a church in what some might describe as a small city, compared to New York, Detroit, or Atlanta, and make it one of the most successful churches in the United States was nothing but God.

The fire damage forced us to look for a place large enough to hold the people who would be in attendance. By the power of God, the largest Jewish Synagogue in New Orleans opened its doors for us to use their facility on Sundays since their worship services were on Saturdays. For the first time in history, Greater St. Stephen was preaching Jesus in the synagogue. Numerous souls came to Christ in that building to the amazement of the public. Soon we had to move to an area school to handle the crowd.

An amazing anointing came over this congregation that had been through a hurricane, a fire, and multiple relocations, yet remained steadfast and immovable in their faith and determination. The devil was attacking the wrong people.

We had good insurance, and we were ready to rebuild in New Orleans, but it was always in my mind that the rebuilt facility would be too small. It was too expensive to rebuild at our largest location, so we sought to sell it to the Fellowship for one dollar and raise the money to rebuild it. That effort failed, but we raised enough money to acquire a group home for the Daughters of the Promise, to house teenage mothers struggling to get through life with their children. God had moved in that venture and it was difficult for us to realize what He was doing.

We called the insurance company with what some would call a "strange" request. We knew the insurance money was supposed to go for the rebuilding of the Uptown location, but our desire was to use the proceeds to rebuild the East location in order to reduce the number of weekly services that we would have had to provide. To our surprise, the company, allowed us to use the funds as we desired and all that remained was to make sure the use of that property as any future collateral would pose no problem.

It was a lot of work but Debra ("Pastor D") led the way. Her first project was to get Greater St. Stephen back "home," because they had been moving from place to place. She first rebuilt Gundy Auditorium at the East location, later renaming it Morton Hall after me. Seating more than one thousand people, it looked better than before Katrina. We marched into that facility in 2009 and returned to the main sanctuary in January of 2010.

Pastor D went even further and led the way in renovating St. Stephen City, a housing development for seventy-five families whose homes had been destroyed in Hurricane Katrina. It is astounding that when God gives you something back, it is always better than before. We were changing forward.

The voice of God told me that Greater St. Stephen in Atlanta needed to change its name. The reason was that the "mother church" was Greater St. Stephen and all of the future churches that we planted would be called Changing a Generation. I decided that this name was for the Atlanta church as well. It became Changing a Generation Full Gospel Baptist Church Atlanta.

Though we had invested $1.3 million in our Atlanta facility, we were still operating under an escalating lease beginning with $28,000 per year and escalating to $36,000 by year four. Recognizing the need for a permanent facility, we located a large church campus that was almost 80 percent complete, but some of the leaders felt it was too expensive to acquire.

The Holy Spirit directed me to go to the site and while peering through the gates, I had such a peace of mind because the Holy Spirit gave me the assurance that this was the place. We would have to expand the sanctuary because it was small and could only seat fifteen hundred. With the finishing out of the class rooms, it would cost about $21 million. We didn't have any money but God was saying "This is it!" I didn't know how we would acquire the money, so I advised our church leadership to "be quiet" about the possibility for fear that someone would try to outbid us for the property.

Out of nowhere, I received a call from Tyler Perry saying that he had heard we were trying to buy the property. I paused for a moment because I couldn't believe that my leaders had broken their promises not to say anything about our interest that quickly. With hesitation, I said "Yes." He went on to tell me that he knew it had to be me. There were two parcels to the property, separated by a man-made lake.

Tyler was interested in one of the parcels of the same property but not the part that we wanted. When he told the property's owners that he was interested in only a portion of the property, their response was that they couldn't entertain an offer because "a church and pastor from New Orleans" were trying to buy it. As far as the owner was concerned, all of the property had to be bought, or none. We would have had to buy all of it and didn't need or want all of it, and the same was true for Tyler. His idea was for us to buy it together.

Caught off guard by his immediate proposal to purchase it together, I brought up the issue of financing the purchase. He immediately said that he was paying cash, which was several million dollars, and that we could let his amount serve as any "down payment." Not having a down payment and not knowing where a down payment would come from, we realized that God had stepped in and supplied it all. This was nothing but God. In this season, we have to believe God no matter how crazy things look.

We were getting assistance with the financing through Evangelical Christian Credit Union (ECCU) out of California. The economy, however, began to take a turn for the worse. The credit union began, in view of what was happening around the country, to back out of its commitments because of the economy. In fact, out of more than two hundred church loans, they kept only seven commitments and we were one of them. Again, it was God.

My life keeps changing in forward, even now. I know a lot of people who use that word, "change," but they really don't mean it. They will try to impress people and try to act like they represent "change," but people who change, change.

I was recently asked what I wanted people to say relating to any legacy that I might leave. My response then, as now, is that I want somebody to say that I made a difference in their lives. I thank God for all the things I have accomplished: able to pastor a successful church, able to found and become presiding Bishop of one of the greatest movements today, to have had a such a great singing career, finding favor in such songs as, "He's Gonna Wipe All Tears Away," "Nothing But the Blood," "Bow Down and Worship Him,"

"Let It Rain," "We Offer Christ," "Let Go, Let God," and "Don't Do It Without Me." The list goes on.

God is God, and God completed the process. We were supposed to be one church in two locations in Atlanta because the burden I still carried was for the people in Decatur. They trusted me and joined because we were on that side of town. Every time we went to that side, people would tell us how they missed our church and how they prayed that one day we would come back.

I thank God that Tyler Perry repurchased some of the land that we owned at Greenbriar and lowered our note to the mortgage company to the point that we were able to take on the obligation of returning to Decatur. The same leasing company that had refused to negotiate before, lowered the price and, in September 2011, we returned to Decatur as well.

In changing forward, keep your integrity. Bind fear, and keep the keys to the kingdom. I'm still celebrating legacy and pursuing destiny. I thank God for my past, but I'm still moving and changing forward.

CHAPTER TWENTY-SIX

YOU CAN CHANGE
FORWARD

G od works in us to desire and do His good pleasure as we embrace His "so that" process and obediently change forward. I thank Him for blessing me, not only with a beautiful wife and family, but also with a strong spiritual family at Greater St. Stephen and Changing a Generation. Beyond this, He has allowed me to raise up anointed spiritual sons and daughters who pastor churches. He has also allowed me to establish the Full Gospel Baptist Church Fellowship. As I look back over my life, I thank God for every challenge to change forward and for giving me a spirit of excellence to lead His people.

When I was young, there were some who came to minister at my father's church who talked down to people. That was the first time I remember saying, "If I ever pastor a church, I want to treat people like I want to be treated." I believe this has been a major key to my success as I've followed the Lord.

It has also been my priority to respect the people God puts under my care and demonstrate God's love for them, even when I have to bring correction. God has brought me a long way: from being the youngest son in a large family with a lot of lessons to learn, to establishing a work that quickly became the "mother eagle" of God's new movement out of tradition and into the fullness of His promises.

I have also learned the importance of being transparent, because people want to know what's on their pastor's or leader's heart. With this in mind, whether you're part of the "full gospel" family or not, I pray my story has encouraged you. I hope my "so that" process has inspired and challenged you, so you know that you can change forward.

You Are an Eagle

If you belong to God you're an eagle too. No matter what difficulties you face, you've been equipped to mount up and soar high above every challenge. I preached a sermon called "The Eagle Stirs Her Nest" from Deuteronomy 32:11-12: "As an eagle stirs up its nest, hovers over its young, spreading out its wings, taking them up, carrying them on its wings, so the LORD alone led him [Jacob/Israel], and there was no foreign god with him."

God has chosen you to be a son or daughter in His kingdom. God has a purpose for you. As you've read this book, I pray God has reminded you of the times He hovered over you, and then spread His wings and carried you. Perhaps you've even had times when you felt the Lord alone led you through difficult situations. I understand this well. Every eagle has these experiences. Such experiences cause us to fly.

The eagle is noted for its superb strength, keenness of vision and unwearied flight. When an eagle encounters a storm, it can soar high above the storm.

So many times when the enemy tried to tell me it was all over for me, God stirred me up so I switched into a second gear and flew high above the storm. I tell everyone in my sphere of influence they can do the same, and right now, that includes you. With God, you too can soar above the storms of life.

The truth about life is that to be at our best and highest, and to reach the goals God has set for us, our "nests" must be disturbed and sometimes even shattered. I'll say it again: To change forward, you have to get out of your comfort zone.

I knew that if I was going to produce a legacy through my spiritual sons and daughters, through my church family, and through the FGBCF, I would have to stretch them out of their nests. I taught them, as I had taught myself: They had to be prepared to confront those challenging places that break up our comfort zones and cast us into the new and untried.

In His wisdom, God loves to allow our nests to be shattered. He knows this will challenge us to change forward. We don't express the fullness of who we are when we're content to live on an "average" level. Eagles are above average. You should never be satisfied with being "average," because remember, this means you're on the top of the bottom. God has called us to be on the top of the top, because He lives inside of us. Greater is He who is in us than he that's in the world.

You may look normal on the outside, but through the power of the Holy Ghost you can operate in the supernatural. You can kick into second gear, rise above the limitations of your mind, and soar in the realm of the spirit. The worst thing that could happen to you is to get scared and never change forward from where you are. Our membership exceeded twenty thousand because I was unafraid to test my wings in unknown spaces.

Now, if you're a pastor, let me encourage you. The only thing God requires of you is to keep growing. Don't get stuck. Be the best you can be. To change forward, you must stretch and challenge yourself. Dare to be different. This may seem hard, even impossible, at times but in God you can do it.

Another fact about eagles: like every living creature, they must eat. Depending on the species of eagle and its location, they eat a variety of things, including snakes. You and I are God's eagles, so we shouldn't be afraid of snakes. We have to let that age-old snake, Satan—our enemy—know he can't rule our space.

The eagle's vision is so clear it can see a snake, a rodent, or even a grasshopper from its lofty place in the sky. My prayer is that you will eat the word of God regularly and heed the voice of God, so you'll see clearly in the spiritual realm and not be afraid to take authority over the enemy.

As spiritual eagles, it's also necessary to watch out for the snakes within. Second Corinthians 10:4-5 teaches that God gives us power to pull down "strongholds" and bring every "thought" captive to the obedience of Christ. The "snake of fear" will try to devour your destiny and purpose. But God has not given you a spirit of fear: "but of power and of love and of a sound mind" (2 Timothy 1:7). The "snake of doubt" will trick you into being "double-minded," so you trust God one day and doubt Him the next. James 1:6-8 teaches us to come to God in faith, without doubting, to ask Him for wisdom; otherwise, we won't receive anything from Him.

The enemy may have many snakes in his arsenal, but God has given us the mighty weapon of His word. He has also given us the Holy Ghost to guide us into all truth and fill us to overflowing with His mighty power. And because of what Jesus—the Word made flesh—has done for you and me on the cross, He triumphed over the enemy and disarmed him for eternity. (See John 1:1-4, 14 and Colossians 2:6-10, 13-15.)

You can change forward! Every time you obey God and tear down an enemy stronghold within, you'll gain strength to see beyond the stormy situations of life.

Always Say Yes to God "So That" You Can Shift and Soar

Always say *yes* to what God has said, because this is how changing forward takes place. Many times when God is in the process of revealing a "new thing" to you, people won't understand. Therefore, you have to learn how to recognize and remain sensitive to His voice. I've been able to keep changing forward because I promised God that I'd never tell Him *no*.

One of our themes for the FGBCF is "Don't Miss the Shift," because God often shifts things into different areas. There were many pastors who started out with me, but missed the shift because they didn't listen closely to the voice of God. Spiritual warfare often comes into our lives because we listen to our own thoughts, and to other people, more than we listen to God.

Changing forward is all about refusing to get stuck in the past by never saying no to what God is saying.

Just remember that God will always speak to you in agreement with His word. This is why I believe there are times we need to fast and pray when we're really seeking the Lord about something we desire. It's very easy to mistake your own ego for God's voice. I also believe wherever God gives vision, He also releases provision. If God is telling you to do something, He's going to make a way. That means you need to trust Him to do it.

A lot of people deal with ego. But remember, God has given you the spirit of power, and of love, and of a *sound mind*. He's going to speak to you and lead you step-by-step through His "so that" process. Having a sound mind means after we hear God, we work through the process by making sound decisions.

This is why it's vital for you to keep drawing near to the Lord and remain sensitive to His voice. The only way you can really know His voice is to spend time talking with Him. You should be seeking Him in prayer daily, not just when you want something.

When you constantly talk to your heavenly Father you'll know His voice so well, that you won't be fooled by another voice. God will give you wisdom.

God Is Working All Things Together for Your Good

There will be many times when you'll have to give up something, willingly let it go "so that" you can change forward. When this happens remember: You can't be filled with two things at one time. You have to be emptied "so that" Christ can fill you with all that He is.

Losing in order to gain has been the story of my life, and no doubt, it has also been your story. Have you reflected on your life as you've read about mine? I hope so. I hope my ups and downs have caused you to take hope in knowing you belong to God, and that He's firmly committed to see you through all the days of your life.

Remember Romans 8:28: "And we know that all things [the good things and the bad things] work together for good to them that love God, to them who are the called according to his purpose" (KJV; emphasis mine). Now, let me restate this for clarity. When we're living according to God's purpose—obeying His voice and changing forward—He works all things together for our good.

Now let me ask: Are you walking in the purpose of God? Have you gotten stuck in the past? Perhaps you've made mistakes, or even had successes, that you simply haven't been able to let go of. If so, it's time to trust God and change forward. Would you pray with me?

Dear heavenly Father, we thank You for sending Jesus to die for our sin, triumph over the enemy, and give us eternal life. We thank You for giving us the gift of the Holy Ghost, so we could be filled with Your power and be Your witnesses in the earth. God, we ask that You help us to change forward. Break the power of those things that have held us captive to the past and have frozen our progress in Your purpose. Speak clearly to us, Lord. Give us hearing ears and obedient hearts. We want to have what You desire for us, and we will let go of anything You require of us. We set our hearts and minds to embrace Your will "so that" we will move into the next level of Your purpose. Mount us up with wings like eagles, Lord. Teach us to soar high above every storm. We thank You for working in us both to desire and do what is pleasing to You, and for giving us victory over the enemy. Father, we'll give You all the glory as we continue changing forward. In Jesus' Name we pray, Amen.

Finally, when God gives you a sense of direction, don't let anything stop you from pursuing it. Keep changing forward. There will be circumstances and people who seek to discourage you from accessing what He has for you.

No matter what may come, it's essential that you stay close to God and keep working toward the best He has for you. Live with excellence. Think big, dream big, and refuse to settle for less. Through all the seasons of my life I have learned this valuable truth: The future is open to those who are open to positive change.

NOTES

1. Spirit over Mind, Not Mind over Spirit

1. Anonymous, "A Christian Confederate Soldier's Prayer," http://thinkexist.com/quotation/i_asked_god_for_strength_that_i_might_ achieve-i/8597.html (accessed May 14, 2012).

5. So New to Me

1. Casietta George, "Walk Around Heaven All Day." Copyright © 1964. Administered by Conrad Music, 6 E 32 St., floor 11, New York, NY 10016-5422. www.bmg.com.

13. Reckless Faith

1. Charles Spurgeon, "Our Omnipotent Leader," *The Evangelization of the World* (London, 1887). http://crupress

.campuscrusadeforchrist.com/green/_assets/crucomm/zwemer thegloryoftheimpossible.pdf (accessed May 14, 2012).

2. Martin Luther King, Jr., "I've Been to the Mountaintop." http://mlk-kpp01.stanford.edu/index.php/encyclopedia/docu mentsentry/ive_been_to_the_mountaintop/ (accessed May 14, 2012).

16. God's Movement

1. John Maxwell, *Developing the Leader Within You* (Nashville: Thomas Nelson, 1993), 388.

17. Losing to Gain

1. John Maxwell, *The 5 Levels of Leadership: Proven Steps to Maximize Your Potential* (New York: Hachette Book Group, 2011).
2. Ibid.
3. Samuel Chand, *Who's Holding Your Ladder?* (Huntley, Ill.: Mall Publishing, 2003).

18. The Collateral Damage of Spiritual Warfare

1. Frank Minirth and Paul Meier, *Happiness Is a Choice: The Symptoms, Causes, and Cures of Depression* (Grand Rapids: Baker Books, 2007).
2. Ibid., 41.